DATE DUE

SEP 2 4 1973			
MAR 3			
9/22/89			
JA 25 '02			
GAYLORD			PRINTED IN U.S.A.

RIOTS, U.S.A.

1765-1965

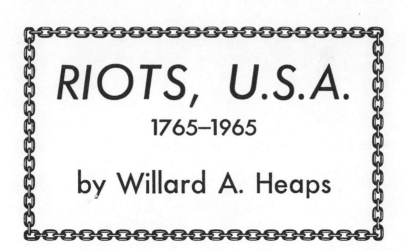

RIOTS, U.S.A.
1765–1965

by Willard A. Heaps

THE SEABURY PRESS · NEW YORK

301.18

ACKNOWLEDGMENTS

Grateful acknowledgment is made to the following publishers and authors for permission to use copyrighted material from the titles listed:

Atheneum Publishers—Theodore H. White, *The Making of the President—1964*. Copyright © 1965 by Theodore H. White. Used by permission of Atheneum Publishers and Jonathan Cape, Ltd.

Harper & Row, Publishers, Incorporated—Martin Luther King, Jr., *Why We Can't Wait*.

Quadrangle Books, Inc.—Martin Oppenheimer and George Lakey, *A Manual for Direct Action*.

The author is particularly grateful to the following authors and publishers for information and unquoted material: Almont Lindsey's *The Pullman Strike* (University of Chicago Press), Richard Moody's *The Astor Place Riot* (Indiana University Press), Elliott M. Rudwick's *Race Riot at East St. Louis* (Southern Illinois University Press), and Leon Wolff's *Lockout* (Harper & Row).

Contents

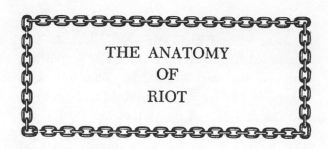

THE ANATOMY
OF
RIOT

1

"WE ARE living in climates of violence," a New York *Herald Tribune* editorial stated after the Los Angeles (Watts) riot in August 1965. Turmoil is everywhere, in many countries throughout the world as well as in our own nation. Ever since the end of World War II a serious discontent has seized the world's people, erupting constantly into protests.

Social scientists studying the outbreaks have written thousands of words in an attempt to define this contemporary spirit of tension. They agree only that a worldwide social revolution is taking place, with explosive manifestations on the streets of cities and towns, on the campuses of colleges and universities, and in front of American embassies throughout the world as well as on Pennsylvania Avenue in front of the White House.

The key word in the explanations of these violent protests is always "dissatisfaction," and it is aggravated dissatisfaction and discontent that foment riots.

The nature and location of contemporary protests appear to have no limits. For the three spring months (March-May) of 1965, for example, the New York *Times* covered twenty-three "riots" in as many foreign countries.

American embassies and consulates were targets in eleven of these violent incidents—in Indonesia (twice), Soviet Russia, Mexico, Japan, Cambodia, Argentina, Venezuela, Chile, Peru, and Colombia. The anti-American mobs ranged in size from five hundred to twenty-five thousand, and the majority of the rioters were students who clashed with both the local police and national soldiers, resulting in many injuries and an occasional death. Buildings were stoned, windows smashed, and several embassies set afire.

Three of the most serious of the spring 1965 riots were against the re-establishment of diplomatic relations. Arabs in Iraq and Lebanon attacked the local embassies of West Germany in protest against that country's diplomatic recognition of Israel. For an entire week in April Korean students clashed repeatedly with police in protest against the renewal of diplomatic relations with Japan, which had occupied Korea from 1910 to 1945.

Tunisians attacked the embassy of the United Arab Republic in protest against slighting remarks made about their President. Africans in Kenya rioted for three days against Asians. Teenage high school students by the thousands rioted in Morocco protesting cutbacks in education. French architectural students in Paris destroyed 350 drawings because of the method by which a competition was judged. Separatist French Canadians in Montreal attempted to stop the observance of Victoria Day, a national holiday.

This was a period when the United States was relatively free from disturbances resulting from organized protests. Even so, fifty-seven Negroes were injured on March 7 in Selma, Alabama, when state police used tear gas, night sticks, and whips to disperse a column of five hundred demonstrators beginning a "freedom walk" to Montgomery, the state capital, to protest voter registration procedures.

Accounts of current riotous protests invariably include common elements—crowds or mobs; slogans shouted and chanted or written on placards and signs; violent physical action such as throwing objects, smashing windows, and attacking cars and persons; and resistance to the agents of law enforcement, whether police or soldiers.

Dictionaries generally list three meanings of the word "riot" when used as a noun. The first definition in its simplest form is "a mass outburst against law and order," and it is this meaning with which we are concerned. Varied sources, however, express this meaning differently, each adding some clarifying and interpretative detail.

For example, Noah Webster's basic definition in his first 1806 dictionary read, "disorderly behavior, tumult." *Webster's New World Dictionary* offers an extended definition: "a wild, violent public disturbance or disturbance of the peace, by a number of persons assembled together."

The standard accepted definition in American common law has remained unchanged since September 12, 1849, when it was stated by Judge Charles P. Daly in the New York City Court of General Sessions. He was presiding at the trial of ten persons charged with riot or conspiracy to riot during the Astor Place riot (Chapter 5). In his charge to the jury Judge Daly first defined unlawful assembly, saying, "Any tumultuous assemblage of three or more persons brought together for no legal or constitutional object, deporting themselves in such manner as to endanger the public peace and excite terror and alarm in rational and firm-minded persons, is unlawful."

Then he added the following to complete the definition of riot: ". . . and whenever three or more persons, in a tumultuous manner, use force or violence in the execution of any design wherein the law does not allow the use of force, they are guilty of riot." This legal definition, then, includes all the elements which make a riot—three or more persons, a gathering for the purpose of enforcing a demand or expressing a protest instead of using due process of law, the use of violence, and the endangering of public peace through terror.

The "three or more," which in actuality is usually a much larger group, may have come together for the specific purpose of expressing their feelings, with no thought of violence or disorder, but when violence is triggered by an inflammatory speech or by a show of opposition and force, most often by the police, the "peaceful assemblage" becomes a riot.

A composite definition of a "mob" might be "a disorderly crowd after its members have lost their sense of individual responsibility and their respect for law." Any crowd or throng can be changed into a mob by agitators. Hotheads, rowdies, riffraff, criminals, and the ever present hangers-on who are always ready to join in any disorder, sometimes seize the initiative and the others blindly follow their lead.

A simple and useful distinction between a crowd, a mob, and a riot is that given by Martin Oppenheimer and George Lakey in *A Manual for Direct Action,* a 1965 publication. In determining what tactics should be used to control demonstrations, the police, according to the authors, need look only at the behavior of the demonstrators: "Is this a crowd, a mob, or a riot? A crowd is just a large group of people; a crowd in motion, usually because of a leader, an incident, the appearance of a hated individual or a symbol, is a mob. A riot is a disturbance by three or more persons who want to overcome opposition to their action by lawful or unlawful means."

The simplest type of crowd in our society is made up of the spectators at a sports event. Most sports fans have already picked a favorite, whether an individual or a team. If a decision is considered unfair by enough people, the crowd may become ugly and a disturbance take place which may turn into a full-scale riot when the crowd becomes an unreasoning mob.

For example, in what *Newsweek* called "the world's worst sporting disaster," at least 318 men, women, and children were killed and 500 injured in a riot at a Peru-Argentina Olympic soccer elimination match at Lima's National Stadium on May 24, 1964.

With Argentina leading 1-0, and two minutes left to play, the referee nullified a Peruvian goal because of a foul. Immediately everything that could be pulled loose in the stadium—cushions, bottles, and even shoes—rained down on the field. Two angered fans then leaped onto the field and started punching the referee, who suspended the game. Many persons in the crowd of forty-five thousand rushed onto the playing field in spite of tear-gas bombs fired by security police.

The fury of the mob in the upper stands meanwhile turned to blind panic as thousands attempted to flee through the nearest exit gates. But they were locked, and before they were broken open hundreds of people were killed or injured by being crushed and trampled in a stampede in the tunnel leading to the gates.

Other parts of the mob broke down a wire fence and poured from the stadium field, smashing shopwindows and setting fire to a dozen cars, a bus, and three buildings nearby. Gangs of rowdies joined in the melee.

Gustave Le Bon, in *The Crowd,* based his observations on the French Revolution, which is the classic example of crowd behavior. Mob action formed the various crises in this upheaval of a people, from 1789 to 1792—the storming of the Bastille, the march on Versailles and the forcible removal of the royal family and the Assembly to Paris, and the storming of the Tuileries palaces and massacre of the Swiss Guards who were protecting Queen Marie Antoinette.

In his study, published seventy years ago, Le Bon first attempted to explain what happens when an ordinary peace-loving individual finds himself in a crowd bent on mischief.

"When the crowd changes into a mob," he wrote, "its individual members lose their identity and merge into a cruel, primitive body which has lost civilized restraints and suddenly has no respect for those law enforcement agencies that resist it."

Le Bon's observation continued: "An isolated individual knows well enough that alone he cannot loot a shop or set fire to a building, and should he be tempted to do so, he will easily and readily resist the temptation. As a part of a mob, however, he becomes conscious of the power he shares with others, and it is sufficient to suggest ideas of pillage, murder, or violence for him to yield immediately to temptation."

Modern psychologists go a step further. They contend that mob action hypnotizes the individual, that he never stops to consider the consequences but merely wants to give in to the urge to do what others are doing and "to get into the act." Subconsciously the individual in the mob is able to release his suppressed desires by doing the things he has always wanted to do but has not dared to do alone.

The appearance of a hated individual or symbol can completely transform a restless crowd into a mob. For example, the display of dismembered corpses and limbs triggered the anti-dissection riot in New York City (Chapter 3). The turning of the drums containing the names of those eligible for the Union Army draft in the offices of the provost marshals started the Draft Riots (Chapter 6). The appearance of the Pinkerton strikebreakers aboard barges on the Monongahela River in front of the Homestead steel mill brought on fatal violence (Chapter 8).

The initial act of violence by crowd members often releases tensions and results in further acts of ever increasing ferocity. Sometimes police action so enrages or antagonizes a crowd that its members resort to unpremeditated violence. Similarly, indecision or ineffective police control action encourages mob defiance. As soon as a crowd realizes that it is stronger than the forces of law and order, the crowd, now a mob, begins to glory in its power and to lose all traces of restraint, leading to ever bolder actions. Many full-scale riots have been prolonged because of the hesitancy of local authorities to summon the aid of outside law enforcement agencies, state or federal. The Pullman strike (Chapter 9) and the Los Angeles (Watts) riot (Chapter 16) are examples.

Psychologists and social scientists interested in crowd behavior point out that most major riots take place during the summer months, particularly during heat waves. Fair weather permits people to congregate and discuss their grievances endlessly. The stifling high humidity undoubtedly serves to fray the nerves of frustrated and angry people. Old and long-festering bitterness and resentments finally erupt into violence. Six of the riots forming chapters in this book occurred in the month of July. The Negro riots during the summers of 1964 and 1965 (Chapter 16) are more recent examples. "Hate and heat" are among the valid causes of these insurrections.

During its growth our American democracy has quite naturally experienced both local and nationwide eruptions. The riots described in this book have been selected to represent the varied types of emotions, prejudices, grievances, frustrations, and problems of living which have led to violence at various times and in different geographical areas. Some may be familiar, others will be new to the reader.

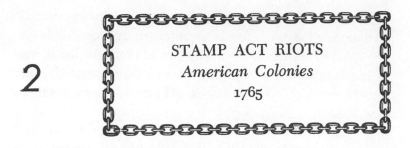

The Riot Road to Revolution

THE FIRST direct tax levied by the English Parliament upon the American colonies was the Stamp Act, passed in March 1765. The resulting protests took the form both of discussion and debate and of widespread outbreaks of violence throughout the colonies, the worst of them taking place in Boston.

For many years before this Boston outbreak of August 1765, the discontent and restlessness which erupted into such violent protest had rankled in the colonists. They had become increasingly involved in the wars of their British masters. The presence of His Majesty's troops was more and more openly resented.

The first sparks to generate the expanding move toward independence were financial. The French and Indian War (Seven Years' War) had been won at an enormous cost to the British, resulting in a huge postwar debt. The necessity of supporting an army in America was a continuous financial burden. New sources of revenue had to be found.

The American Revenue Act of 1764, popularly called

9

the Sugar Act, was the first law ever passed by the British
Parliament for the specific purpose of raising funds in
the colonies for the Crown. The Act not only added items
to the existing list of dutiable imports but increased, and
sometimes doubled, the levies. At the same time other
new laws strengthened customs enforcement.

The Americans immediately realized that their colonial
economy might well collapse. Boston, then a city of 20,-
000, vied with New York and Philadelphia for commercial
supremacy, and the first protests were not long in coming
from that city's merchants. A town meeting on May 24,
1764, denounced the new measures; it was here that lawyer James Otis coined the slogan "No taxation without
representation!" The meeting also proposed action by the
colonies in protest.

This united objection came into full-blown strength
with the passage of the Stamp Act. If the yield met expec-
tations, the Act would produce sufficient funds to pay
one third of the upkeep of the colonial military forces.
The tax was placed upon newspapers, pamphlets, broad-
sides, legal documents, licenses, and even dice and playing cards. The receipts were to be paid into the "defense
fund" of the colonies. To ease the blow, Americans were
to be appointed as stamp agents or masters, as they were
called.

The chorus of opposition was immediate. Direct taxation was new, and many felt that this would be followed
by still further levies. Everyone was affected, even groups
who carried great weight, such as lawyers, printers, merchants, and shipowners.

During the spring of 1765 several colonial legislatures
expressed strenuous objections. In Virginia's House of

Burgesses, Patrick Henry delivered a fiery speech. Strong evidence indicates that he ended with an apology for his defiant and almost treasonable words rather than with the ringing declaration "If this be treason, make the most of it!" with which he has been credited. But after his speech several resolutions expressed the Virginia opposition.

This impending tax burden was so offensive that during the summer secret organizations known as the Sons of Liberty were formed throughout the colonies for the specific purpose of organizing the opposition to the Stamp Act. When necessary, this took the form of calculated mass violence. Mobs terrified the appointed tax masters into resigning.

The Act was to enter into force on November 1. Two and a half months before, in mid-August, riots broke out in Boston. When news reached the city that Andrew Oliver, secretary of the Massachusetts Bay Province, would be asked to serve as stamp distributor there, a mob carefully organized by the local Sons of Liberty staged a riot against him—this even before his appointment. Early on the morning of August 14 effigies labeled to represent "The Stamp Officer" and "The Devil" were hung from a huge elm known as the Great Tree. A curious crowd gathered and news of the spectacle spread rapidly. By sundown, at the end of the workday, "a great concourse of people" followed a procession of six men carrying the images on a bier. Forty easily recognized prominent Whig citizens, thinly disguised in the clothes of mechanics, headed the marchers. Shouting "Liberty! No stamps!" they marched to the building which was to be the office of the stamp master. This they demolished "in no time at all," with not a brick of the wall left standing.

Bearing pieces of wood from the wreckage, the mob went on to Fort Hill, kindled a huge bonfire, and burned the two figures in effigy.

But the main target was the nearby house of the luckless Oliver. Chief Justice Thomas Hutchinson and the sheriff of Suffolk County awaited the rioters, and when they tried to persuade the mob to disperse they were answered with a volley of stones. The windows were all smashed, the furniture wrecked, and the walls defaced, while outside the fence was torn down, the barn leveled, and the garden torn up and trampled. The following day, as anticipated, the terrified Oliver resigned the commission he had not yet received. Though the governor offered a reward of one hundred pounds for the conviction of anyone involved in the disturbance, no one was identified or arrested.

The Great Tree became known as the Liberty Tree, and speakers thereafter customarily harangued mobs under its branches before sending them out on missions.

Many of the riots were deliberately engineered by Whig leaders. The behind-the-scenes maneuvering and strategy planning by merchants, lawyers, and planters were unique in that for the first time "respectable" people not only fomented riots but actually participated in them. Boston leaders like Samuel Adams, and John Hancock, the town's principal merchant, made no effort to conceal their manipulations and were present and recognized in several street uprisings and riots.

The street rioters for the most part were ordinary citizens who responded readily to the inciting tirades of leaders. They were then eager to wreak vengeance upon those at hand, who were more readily available than the officials in the mother country—its agents, governors, customs officers, or stamp distributors.

The Boston riot of August 14, 1765, proved to be only a preface to violence in that city. Less than a fortnight later, on the twenty-sixth, a mob led by shoemaker Ebenezer Mackintosh, one of the leaders of the notorious South Side gang who specialized in organizing crowds of workingmen for protest demonstrations, was assembled under the Great Tree. In anticipation of a riotous outbreak, a law officer was dispatched to read the Riot Act to them.

This ceremony of reading the Riot Act was adopted in the colonies as a routine in law enforcement. The 1715 law had been enacted in Great Britain during the reign of George I when lawless outbreaks of the Jacobite opposition to the British monarchy were so frequent and dangerous that special measures were required to curb the demonstrations against the Crown.

The so-called Riot Act made it a felony for a rioter to refuse to obey the command of a lawful authority to disperse. The text provided that "if twelve or more persons are unlawfully assembled to the disturbance of public peace they must disperse on proclamation or be held guilty of felony." The "proclamation" was the Act itself.

In case of disturbances in Great Britain and the American colonies, such as the Boston crowd action, a law officer accompanied by a detachment of His Majesty's troops would proceed to the scene of the disorder. There he would read the entire text of the Act, with its full legal terminology. This required about five minutes. Since the mobs were generally noisy and highly excited, the reading of the text in most cases could not be heard above the confusion; citizens were quite familiar with its contents and purpose, and paused only when they feared action by the soldiers for their inattention.

The law commanded the group to disperse peacefully within an hour after the reading. The troops would then withdraw to await developments. Surprisingly enough, the Riot Act was in most cases effective, though the gift of time—sixty precious minutes—it granted was often sufficient for the accomplishment of much mischief.

On this August day the crowd gathered under the Great Tree listened in bored but respectful silence, for they knew that within the hour given them to disperse before being arrested they would be engaged on their planned mischief in another part of town, having "peaceably departed" according to the wording of the Act.

Within two hours this mob had attacked the house and first-floor office of the register of the Vice Admiralty Court, destroying all records and papers in a huge bonfire. The next victim was the comptroller of customs, their target his recently completed residence where, in the words of a contemporary account, "after tearing down the fences, breaking the windows, etc., they at length entered the house and in the most savage and destructive manner broke and abused the furniture, chairs, tables, desks, glasses, china, and, in short, everything they could lay their hands on; at the same time purloining his money and dispersing his private books and papers." Other accounts noted that they obviously enjoyed the contents of his wine cellar.

Mackintosh's men had held the stage during the afternoon and early evening. Now it was time for the absent workingmen who had been occupied at their places of employment. The wrath of these ordinary citizens found vehement expression during the evening. The objective of the mob's wrath was Lieutenant Governor Thomas Hutchinson, who was also Chief Justice of the Massachusetts Bay Province. He had opposed the Stamp Act but had made the mistake of attempting to prevent the destruction of the house of Andrew Oliver, his brother-in-law, a fortnight before. His attempt was interpreted to mean that the governor would lend support to the future collections. The large crowd, however, was unable to vent its fury upon Hutchinson because, fortunately for him, he had been forewarned and was able to escape with his family.

The massive Hutchinson mansion was one of the finest examples of architecture in all the colonies, fronted with Ionic columns and surmounted by a large cupola. Smashing the heavy doors with broadaxes, the rioters swept into the house and remained throughout the night, gutting it from ground to roof. Hutchinson's own account described their work: "They destroyed, carried away, or cast into the street, everything that was in the house; demolished every part of it, except the walls as far as lay in their power, and even began to break away the brick work." They slashed the paintings to shreds, smashed dinnerware piece by piece, ripped the carpets into strips, and cut up the silk and brocade wall coverings. His books and private papers were thrown into the street. A great collection of manuscripts on the history of Massachusetts Bay was burned. The handwritten manuscript of the second volume of his history of the Colony was scattered in the mud —but later recovered and reassembled.

When the interior was wrecked, several men climbed

to the roof and after three hours were finally able to remove the cupola and send it smashing to the ground. The construction of the roof, however, was so solid that they could not uncover much of it before daylight. Others had meanwhile cut down or broken the branches of the apple trees on the grounds.

The night's work was thorough, and even the most rabid opponents of the Stamp Act felt that strong measures should be taken to prevent a recurrence of such disorders. A town meeting deplored the violence, condemned the rioters, and offered the usual rewards for identification of participants. None were ever punished. The chief instigator, Mackintosh, was not arrested because of threats that more riots would result. The six or seven who were jailed were freed before their trials by a crowd who forced the jailer to give up the keys. The peace of Boston was not again disturbed for several years.

The violence of protest in the twelve other colonial provinces did not match Boston in destruction. The principal purpose of the crowds gathered by the Sons of Liberty was to obtain the forced resignations of the stamp agents through intimidation and harassment rather than rack and ruin. Most appointees were happy to resign their commissions publicly. Those who were brave (or stubborn) enough to resist the threats of local crowds found it necessary to flee for their lives. Zachariah Hood of Maryland was a victim of mob action: his store was completely plundered and torn down, he was burned in effigy. When he escaped to seek refuge in New York he rode so hard that he killed his horse on the road. The hiding place of the tormented man was discovered by the New York Sons of Liberty, who forced his resignation *in absentia.*

The Virginia stamp master returned from London to discover that he was the most unpopular citizen in the colony; he lost no time in abandoning his new post. A mob forced the New Hampshire agent not only to resign but to burn his commission publicly. The Rhode Island appointee escaped mob action only because he did not own the house in which he lived. The crowd was content instead to wreck the Newport houses of two wealthy vocal supporters of the Stamp Act.

A more united and legal mode of protest was taken by the Stamp Act Congress in October, when representatives of nine colonies listed their objections and dispatched them to London. Another peaceful method of protest was the application of economic boycotts; scores of merchants banned the purchase of British goods, and this virtual embargo resulted in huge financial losses for the mother country.

The arrival of the stamps at various ports was unpublicized and most were concealed to avoid further mob action; besides, there were no agents to receive them.

London was deaf to all protests, and the Stamp Act became effective as planned on November 1. No widespread disturbances marked the date, for the colonists had already signified their intention of refusing to obey the Act. Only in New York City was there a full-scale riot.

That city was the headquarters of the British army in North America. Since the army was to be responsible for the enforcement of the Act should the rebellion become open, the presence of the soldiers was strongly resented. Part of this dislike was brought about by the tactlessness of those in command. The ranking colonel, whose home was in the British fox-hunting region, had often declared that he was eager to take up "the sport of hunting down American rebels." With unparalleled tactlessness he had declared that he would "cram the stamps down their throats" with his sword.

On the evening of November 1 about three thousand men—waterfront workers, laboring men, and sailors—carrying effigies of the lieutenant governor and the devil, took their stand at the gate of Fort George, the army headquarters. The garrison soldiers wisely withheld their fire in spite of the insults and curses shouted at them and the dares to open fire. The citizens beat upon the gate and walls with sticks, creating a terrible racket.

When these annoyances brought no response, the crowd burned the lieutenant governor's coach along with his effigy. Then the local Sons of Liberty streamed to the house of the offensive and hated colonel, forced their way in, and stripped it of the contents to make a huge bonfire.

The protests during the Stamp Act crisis were the first example of united colonial action against Great Britain as a preliminary step toward independence. Because of this defiance the Act was never enforced and was repealed in March 1766.

An insurrection is an uprising against established law; a rebellion is an uprising against established government. The 1765 riots were both. The beginning of any insurrection and rebellion leading to an eventual full-scale revolution is almost always marked by scattered riots when the grievances of citizens are not adjusted and they become exasperated beyond further endurance. These riots were the beginning of the overt protests of the colonists which marked their road to revolution.

DOCTORS' RIOT

New York City

April 13-14, 1788

Revenge on the Body Snatchers

IN 1788 New York City was the capital of the newly
independent colonies, and George Washington was to
be inaugurated there as the first President of the United
States a year later when the Constitution was ratified.
The population was a little over 25,000, and they lived
in three thousand houses. The entire "city" lay south of
what is now Washington Square, at the foot of Fifth
Avenue, which was in open country. The select residential
district centered around Wall Street, and Broadway was
the principal thoroughfare.

Medical students received training at King's College
(later Columbia College), the courses beginning in 1768.
The most important center for anatomy studies in postwar
New York City was the New York Hospital, where Richard Bayley, a former physician in the British army who
had received training under the celebrated Scottish anat-
omist John Hunter, had established a museum of specimens and directed laboratory dissection of human bodies.

At that time bodies of the dead could not be obtained

legally, and so the students, under cover of darkness, secretly stole corpses from two cemeteries, the potter's field and the Negro burial ground, where the bodies buried in common graves, without coffins, could easily be dug up and carried away. Each student was required to supply a corpse for his sole use in dissection, and by early 1788 grave robbing, or body snatching as it was popularly known, had become common and students bolder. When in February a group took a body from the graveyard of Trinity Church, the oldest in the city, public indignation mounted.

Throughout that spring the medical students, though severely criticized in the two weekly newspapers, continued their activities recklessly while public anger increased. The reports were exaggerated by countless rumors, and everyone recalled the harrowing details of the grave-robbing epidemic in Scotland and England during the first half of the century.

Local bitterness increased until an unfortunate and tactless incident on April 13 precipitated the two-day Doctors' Riot, alternately termed the Anti-Dissection Riot.

That Sunday afternoon was sunny and mild. Several medical students and physicians were dissecting a cadaver under the direction of their instructor, Dr. Bayley, in the laboratory of the New York Hospital on the west side of Broadway at Duane Street. The room had recently been painted and the ladders of the workmen lay on the ground below. The windows were open to allow the escape of the odors of the paint and of the formaldehyde in which the corpses had been preserved. A group of small boys were playing on the lawn below.

Led by curiosity, one of the lads placed a ladder against

the wall, climbed up to a window of the laboratory, and peered in. The students had been plagued and annoyed by other curious Peeping Toms, and their patience had become strained.

The students were working together on a female cadaver and, according to one report, one of them happened at that very moment to hang an arm to dry on a line suspended in the windowframe. Another report asserted that a doctor-student named John Hicks waved the arm at the boy to frighten him off. A third account maintained that the annoyed Dr. Hicks tactlessly brandished the arm in the lad's face, at the same time shouting, "This is your mother's arm; get off the ladder or I'll hit you with it," or some similar remark. The boy fled in terror, rushing to his home where he breathlessly told the story to his father, a stonemason.

By an uncanny and one-in-a-million coincidence, it so happened that the boy's mother *had* actually died a few weeks before. The distraught father rounded up some friends and visited her grave. To their horror they discovered that the casket had been broken open and was empty.

The outraged men rushed to gather a party of their fellow workmen, who armed themselves with the tools of their trade. The shocking news, enlarged upon with each repetition, spread like wildfire, and a large mob assembled. As they moved up Broadway their number swelled with sympathetic, aroused bystanders. The doctors and most of the students in the hospital had been forewarned and were able to escape before the crowd burst open the locked door of the south wing.

Pouring into the building, the mob, which may have

numbered a thousand, first came upon the choice collection of imported anatomical specimens, the best in the country—skeletons, bones of different body parts, various chemically preserved organs in glass containers, wax models, and dry, injected human specimens. These they smashed to bits and totally destroyed.

At the same time some of the throng broke into the dissecting rooms. Finding several incompletely dissected bodies, they "seized upon the fragments, heads, legs, arms, and trunks, and exposed them from the windows and doors to public view," while screaming oaths and vows of vengeance. The observers outside were thus whipped into an equal fury which increased when these body portions were brought out, heaped into carts, and carried away for identification and reburial.

Some of the mob broke down the door of the room in which four of the students had taken refuge. But they were saved by the timely arrival of Mayor James Duane with Sheriff Robert Boyd and several prominent citizens. With hisses and howls of the crowd ringing in their ears, the students were taken across the fields to the jail, then in City Hall Park, where they were held for safekeeping under the protection of the regular guards and a few hastily summoned militiamen. Most of the other students and many of the town's doctors also sought refuge in the jail on Sunday evening and the next morning.

If the mayor's party believed that the incident had ended, they were mistaken. On Monday morning a crowd, this time with fresh reinforcements including sailors, loafers, criminals, and motley mischief-makers, assembled at the hospital. They were determined to search the houses of all the city's physicians, of which there were twenty-five, in order to locate other corpses which had been reported as stolen.

Governor George Clinton and Mayor Duane realized the seriousness of the situation and decided to make a personal appeal to the crowd. After reading the Riot Act, they attempted to persuade the throng to disperse and use no violence. They promised that a thorough official investigation would be made of all reported grave robberies and that the guilty would be punished under the law. These appeals and promises appeared to satisfy some of the crowd, and they left.

But the greater part refused to be pacified; they wanted to locate the missing corpses themselves, and so began their searches. A visit to the medical rooms of King's College revealed nothing. While the governor and mayor, who had accompanied the crowd, continued to plead for restraint at each spot, individual searches of the offices and homes of several doctors were undertaken by smaller groups who gave reports to the crowds waiting outside. But the searches soon proved both unexciting and unrewarding, and one by one the groups dispersed.

Now the doctors themselves became the targets of the crowd's displeasure. Early in the afternoon about four hundred citizens assembled outside the city jail, with the avowed purpose of taking vengeance upon the doctors and students locked within. With loud shouts and yells they began the cadenced cry, "Bring out the doctors! Bring out the doctors!" They threatened to tear down the three-story building unless their quarries were surrendered to them.

Thoroughly alarmed, the intended victims and their companion-prisoners, vagrants and criminals, barricaded the doors and windows and armed themselves with the weapons available. Sheriff Boyd attempted to remonstrate with the crowd, but they would have nothing to do with him and continued their shouted demands.

The authorities felt that a show of force was now imperative. Inasmuch as the city in those days did not possess police in numbers sufficient to cope with the situation, a small military force was hastily organized. By three o'clock in the afternoon the eighteen-man detachment marched up Broadway. Unpredictably, the crowd at the jail permitted them to pass to the entrance, while showering them with dirt and stones accompanied by taunts, jeers, and mocking laughter. But the soldiers wheeled about and marched away; their intention had evidently been to intimidate the crowd enough to prevent violence.

Half an hour later another small party of a dozen men was dispatched to the jail. As the little handful marched up, the crowd broke into boisterous laughter and rushed to meet them. "Swarming like bees around them, the rabble snatched away their muskets and broke them into pieces on the pavement." The soldiers fled in full retreat.

This first successful act of open resistance excited the rioters still more. Then the storm broke. Amid shouts of "To the jail! To the jail!" the crowd, which had swelled to an estimated five thousand, determined to force an entrance by rushing against the doors in an attempt to unhinge them. The heavy bolts and bars withstood the onslaught.

Smashing the windows with stones, a few attackers

attempted to enter through them, but they were beaten back by the handful of men inside. The thwarted assailants now armed themselves with pickets—every fence within blocks of the jail was destroyed to provide weapons for the mob—and, advancing with these, made renewed desperate efforts to clear the windows. But those inside repulsed them. One man was bayoneted as he climbed through a broken window. The fight continued until dusk, amid yells, shouts, and a veritable tumult of noises.

Mayor Duane had already realized that stern measures were urgently necessary in order to disperse the crowd, and Governor Clinton now agreed to call out the militia. But only fifty men could be assembled; the rest were in the mob.

It became necessary then to round up any available experienced soldiers, and these were joined by prominent citizens who might lend prestige to the force and effectively reason with the mob. Among the volunteers armed with swords and clubs were John Jay, Alexander Hamilton, who had just completed work on his half of the *Federalist* papers, and retired Baron Friedrich Von Steuben, who had contributed so much to the organization of the Continental (colonial) Army.

Night had fallen by the time the military unit moved to the jail. "In the dim starlight their bayonets were seen gleaming as they marched steadily forward on the dark, heaving mass that filled the street as far as the eye could see," read a newspaper account. The company approached the waiting mob, which took no action until the soldiers were "within ten paces of the jail door." Then, believing that the militiamen were under orders either not to fire or to fire over their heads, the crowd, yelling screams of defiance, commenced to throw brickbats, stones, and sticks.

A concerted attack knocked down and badly wounded several in the group of civilians. Jay, severely injured by a brick thrown into his carriage, was in bed with a concussion for ten days afterward. Hamilton was struck by a stone, and Mayor Duane was beaten on the head, knocked down, and trampled on.

While Baron Von Steuben was shouting to Governor Clinton above the din, urging him not to quell the riot with firearms, he was struck on the forehead by a well-aimed paving stone thrown with such force that he was knocked down. His attitude changed: as he fell bleeding to the street, he called out loudly, "Fire, Governor, fire!"

The commanding officer immediately shouted the order "Ready . . . aim . . . fire!" The crowd had not expected this close, point-blank volley, and they stopped in amazement and hesitation as five rioters fell dead and seven or eight wounded dropped to the pavement.

Instead of waiting to see whether the mob would disperse, the commander ordered another round. As more of their companions fell, the rioters stood still for a long moment, almost suspended in shocked bewilderment, before advancing on the soldiers and forcing them to retreat. The armed guards, soldiers, and civilians within the jail now began to discharge their muskets through the windows, adding to the dangerous situation of the surrounded soldiers, three of whom were killed by this gunfire or the missiles of the rioters. The soldiers now fixed bayonets and held off the mob while they continued to fall back down Broadway until they reached St. Paul's Church. There they turned and again charged the crowd, striking some of them with the backs of their sabers, pursuing them into the churchyard burial ground, and finally succeeding in dispersing them.

The crowd remaining in front of the jail now broke up and fled in all directions, clearing the street and grounds in a few minutes. The wounded were cared for, the dead carried away, and troops guarded the jail throughout the night.

While the afternoon disturbances were occupying the mob at the jail, other smaller groups set out to terrorize the few doctors and medical students remaining in the city. Physicians were forced to "slip out of windows, creep beneath bean barrels, flee to rooftops, crawl up chimneys, and hide behind feather beds." Those who had not accepted the sheriff's offer of protection fled from the city in closed carriages.

When the search parties found no corpses, a thwarted few smashed the equipment and furniture in the doctors' offices and homes.

In order to maintain order by continuing the show of force, state militia units in the surrounding countryside were ordered to form and march into the city. Two detachments, a brigade of foot soldiers and a regiment of artillery, responded. The sight of these units marching through the streets prevented the formation of mobs. A large number of people gathered in front of the jail, looking with horror at the bloodstained pavement. They cursed and threatened the soldiers stationed outside, who quietly stood at attention, quite ready to open fire at any attempted violence or breach of peace.

A full-dress parade held later in the day, with all the militia detachments marching in full force, served to quench any remaining riotous spirit. Even so, the city seethed with excitement for several days and it was evident that peace was maintained only through fear of the military. The doctors, teachers, and students were still considered the cause of the tragic disturbances. Those suspected or known to be practicing dissection began to maintain their innocence of grave robbing. This they did by inserting paid notices in the newspapers wherein they one and all deplored the unfortunate events and avowed that they had not used stolen bodies for their studies.

In his charge to the grand jury convened within two days to investigate the disorder, Mayor Duane condemned the body snatchers and promised to press for their punishment. He also denounced the citizens for "an offense striking at the very foundation of all government and security—rushing into riot and violence, and obstinately persisting even to occasion the shedding of blood."

The grand jury investigation resulted in penalties for the doctors and students, though none were punished by the Court. The New York Hospital's Board of Governors dismissed from its staff and student body all those in the dissecting room on that fatal Sunday afternoon, and assessed individual fines of £22.7.10 against each offender, today equal in purchasing power to the sum of twenty dollars.

As a result of the New York City Doctors' Riot, the first

American law to aid anatomy study was passed during the Twelfth Session of the New York State Senate and Assembly in the winter and spring of 1788-89. This law made it legal for the courts to add dissection to the death penalty in cases of murder, arson, and burglary. A limited supply of "legal" cadavers was therefore available. These Anatomy Acts of 1789 both legally authorized dissection and specifically spelled out punishment for grave robbers.

In 1790 the First Congress of the United States passed legislation similar to the New York State law of the previous year. Doctors and teachers in individual states, however, still encountered a great deal of difficulty in legally securing sufficient bodies, and body snatching continued in rural areas well into the 1800s. But in more modern times public enlightenment, in spite of strong anti-dissection opposition, has made the legal supply ample.

ANTI-CATHOLIC RIOTS
Philadelphia
May 6-8, July 5-8, 1844

Prejudice in the
City of Brotherly Love

RELIGIOUS intolerance and prejudice in our country's history are particularly ironic because the first colonists came to enjoy freedom of religious worship—a freedom stated in Article I of the Bill of Rights, the First Amendment to the Constitution.

Anti-Catholicism was particularly rampant following the tremendous influx of Irish immigrants during the 1830s. By 1840 more than forty per cent of the foreign-born in the United States were Irish. And these Irish were overwhelmingly Catholic.

The opposition stemmed from ignorance. It was asserted and seriously believed that the loyalty of the Irish would be owed to Rome and the Pope rather than to their new country and that cheap Irish labor would lower the American standard of living. The "shanty" element were undesirable as citizens, their enemies contended, because they were intemperate, quarrelsome, and clannish.

For more than a decade before the 1840s, anti-Catholic

feeling had been fostered by many societies, lecturers, newspapers, and Protestant clergymen. Even a political party, the American Republicans, was formed to protect "native American" interests. A campaign to discredit Catholics was fostered by the American Protestant Association, and in Philadelphia its members spread the rumor of papal intentions to seize control of the city.

A controversy over classroom Bible reading shook Philadelphia to its very foundations in 1842. School Bible reading was required by law. Bishop Francis Kenrick had maintained that it was unjust to make Catholic children listen to the Protestant (King James) version of the Scriptures. He asked the school board to excuse Catholic students from religious instruction and to permit the use of the Catholic (Douay) version. The request was granted, and the heat of the subsequent discussion brought out all the ugliness inherent in religious prejudice and bigotry. In 1844 the City of Brotherly Love was shaken by a series of riots difficult to match for sheer bitterness and violence.

The American Republicans, popularly called Nativists, had twisted Bishop Kenrick's request into an insult on the Bible itself. They held street meetings at which the most violent verbal tirades were thundered against Catholics, almost inviting the Irish to attack.

On the afternoon of May 6, 1844, a well-publicized gathering "peaceably" assembled in the heavily Irish Kensington section, several thousand strong. Rain drove them to a neighboring hall. A fight started there and spread to the street, where muskets and guns were discharged by Irishmen from the roofs, windows, and doors. The Nativists replied with stones and bricks, but before they were driven away one of their number, a young marcher who became the martyr of the riots, was killed and many others wounded. An indignation memorial meeting in the evening ended in a pitched battle which was broken up by the militia.

Excitement in the city reached fever heat and further "action" was called for by both sides. The next afternoon the Nativists held another meeting, passed resolutions, denounced the Catholics, and, inflamed by their own oratory, decided to adjourn in a body to the scene of the previous day's riot. The parade, complete with drums and the soiled and torn American flag on which was painted, "This is the flag that was trampled by Irish Papists," was met by volleys fired at them from the house of an Irish fire company. Several were killed and wounded. But the Nativists broke in the door, dragged out the hose carriage, and destroyed it under heavy fire.

After a strategic retreat the anti-Catholics returned in the evening and applied the torch to the firehouse. The flames, unchecked because the mob refused to let firemen approach the district, engulfed more than thirty houses and buildings belonging to Irishmen. Only the arrival of a militia brigade toward midnight put an end to the appalling destruction. The evening's Nativist toll was eight killed and forty wounded by the Irish.

All was calm on the morning of the eighth of May, for the sight of the patrolling troops sobered everyone. But when the word was spread that the militiamen had been ordered not to fire on the people, Kensington was again attacked by a maddened crowd which swept from street to street like locusts, setting fire to houses, regardless of ownership, at random. Houses were searched for arms before being burned. In midafternoon St. Michael's Catholic Church and an adjoining convent were burned to the ground, the unchecked flames spreading to two rows of houses. All the Irish in the section had by then fled, and the militia dispersed the rioters.

The Nativist mob returned to the heart of the city. By now the bishop had urged the city's Catholics to remain peaceful and not attempt to defend their churches. Few could believe that church buildings would continue to be the targets of Nativist wrath. The mayor awaited the Nativists at St. Augustine's Church and held their attention long enough to assure them that the building was undefended.

This was indeed welcome news and the crowd broke open the doors and set the church on fire. The flames engulfed the structure and lit the sky with a brilliant glow. Mounting rapidly, they soon consumed the roof and the wooden cupola surmounted by a gilded cross. When the cross fell crashing to the ground, cheer after cheer burst from the observers.

While men shrieked their approval and delight, a troop of mounted militia galloped up but was afraid to deal with the mob which so greatly outnumbered them. The adjoining schoolhouse was plundered. The books in its valuable library were thrown out of the windows and kicked into heaps, forming huge bonfires. The building was then burned. By morning nothing was left but a mass of ruins inside blackened walls.

This outrage marked the peak of mob rule. The city authorities began to realize the seriousness of the situa-

tion and the extent of danger should stronger measures
not be taken. A force of citizen police was enrolled to
patrol the streets both day and night. The governor dispatched additional militia troops to Philadelphia. The
bishop closed all the Catholic churches. Peace had apparently been restored. The animosity of the anti-Catholics had seemingly calmed down.

Nevertheless, the belief persisted that the riots were a
form of zealous crusade. The American Republicans became the Native American Party and membership increased rapidly. Meetings attracted huge crowds. The
Bible-reading controversy was renewed and tempers again
simmered.

The breaking point came on the Fourth of July. Seventy
thousand Nativists paraded in a patriotic "American"
demonstration, carrying banners which bore inflammatory
slogans. The widows and orphans of victims of the May
riots rode in carriages, an unfortunate reminder of what
might well have been left as a painful incident of the past.

By evening of the next day uneasy groups were milling
about; they finally focused their combined attention on
the Church of St. Philip of Neri in suburban Southwark.
Guns and powder had been stored in the building for
possible use should the holiday paraders turn to violence.
The mob was on the brink of searching the church when
the sheriff arrived and calmed them by making an official
survey and bringing out twelve muskets. A search by a
committee of twenty appointed on the spot revealed an
additional seventy-five guns and a large supply of ammunition guarded by several armed men.

The crowd was not told of this discovery and dispersed
at midnight when soldiers arrived. But such a secret could

not long be kept, and by midmorning a crowd almost routinely gathered at St. Philip's to protest. The sheriff and his posse cleared the street in front of the church. For the rest of the day the militia stood guard in the area. A part of the mob stoned a detachment. By this time the patience of the commander was nearly exhausted, for his men were continually taunted and insulted. He gave the order that the soldiers should fire a small cannon if the mob again attempted to mount the church steps. Charles Naylor, one of the sheriff's posse, harangued the soldiers and countermanded the order. For this he was arrested and held inside the church under guard of an Irish military company. This situation was scarcely calculated to calm the crowd but they feared the cannon and so broke up shortly after dark—not, however, before their leader issued an ultimatum that they would remove Naylor by force if he were not released by noon of the next day.

All Catholic churches had been closed and St. Philip's was still under heavy guard on Sunday, July 7. The Nativist crowd, substantially increased in numbers, assembled early and reminded the soldiers of their noon deadline. They had borrowed two cannons and a supply of gunpowder from ships at the wharves and now placed these at the entrance in front of the guards. The commander was determined that he would not be intimidated, and just before twelve o'clock he publicly refused to surrender the prisoner.

This was the moment when the crowd of anti-Catholics gathered in front of the Church of St. Philip of Neri went mad. First they broke the windows on all sides, but they were too high to be reached without ladders. The order was given to fire the cannon, but the powder was wet and nothing happened. Undaunted, some men obtained a log and, using this as a battering ram, broke down the doors of the church. The leader found Naylor and triumphantly bore him outside, where he was cheered again and again.

But they had also seen the Irish unit, the Hibernia Greens. A demand was issued: unless the military company was removed, the church would be burned. Within minutes the Greens marched outside, to be greeted with catcalls and boos. One of the company turned, fired, and shot a boy, whereupon they were assaulted with stones, bricks, sticks, and assorted missiles. They broke ranks and fled for their lives after at least one had been killed and several injured.

The spreading report that Irish troops had fired on Protestant citizens produced renewed excitement. Brushing aside those who were urging calm, crowds rushed into the church and were prevented from setting fire to it only by the presence of armed members of their fellow American Republicans on guard there. Instead they established themselves triumphantly, as in a fortress that had been carried by storm.

The milling crowd outside, which was increasing by the moment, burst into violence without any warning. The law authorities realized that the strongest possible measures were necessary. By late afternoon a company of troops cleared the church and the square in front of it, erecting barricades and placing cannons at each of the approaching streets. A second company en route to the scene was attacked and its confused commander gave an order to fire. A single volley left seven citizens dead and a score wounded.

New crowds assembled to revenge this latest outrage. Another cannon and a quantity of muskets were obtained, and after dark the rioters fired point-blank at the soldiers near the door. The military force answered and a pitched battle raged for several hours. The crowd loaded the cannon again and again with ammunition (and later with bolts, chains, and spikes) and fired muskets with such careless aim that some of their own number were wounded or killed. From upper-story windows and roof-tops the rioters shot at soldiers below. They even stretched ropes across the streets to halt the cavalry should they approach in the darkness.

The soldiers, hemmed in on every side, held their ground and used their own two cannons. Both sides seemed resolved to continue the battle throughout the night if necessary. The soldiers' ammunition was almost used up when a company of state troops arrived and forced the mob to give way after they had captured the cannon. By midnight the firing had ceased and by dawn the streets were clear.

Peace was restored to the City of Brotherly Love. The total number of dead and wounded—of anti-Catholics, Irish, and soldiers—was never agreed upon. The Nativists at the time fixed the toll of both sides at thirteen killed and fifteen injured. Later (and more reliable) figures were given as from twenty to twenty-four dead and "more than a hundred" wounded; these numbers were never analyzed.

The excitement and the bitter passions unleashed during the six days of May and July could not be expected to die down at once. The mayor sensed the continued hostility of the Protestant citizens against the soldiers and

ordered them withdrawn. They were replaced at the
church by citizen guards. Many thousands of Catholics
who had left Philadelphia began cautiously to return,
one by one. The governor spoke at several scattered
points, urging peace; on his order more than five thousand troops were pouring into the city. And for days the
main topic of conversation was the riots and the blame
for them.

Official inquiries unanimously blamed the Catholics for
provoking the disturbances. A city investigating committee blamed the May riots entirely on the Irish, who had
"broken up a peaceful procession of American citizens."
The June grand jury ascribed the trouble to "the efforts
of a portion of the community to exclude the Bible from
our public schools" and the fact that "meetings were
rudely disturbed and fired upon by a band of lawless,
irresponsible men, some of whom had resided in our
country only for a short period." A second grand jury
blamed the July riots solely on the Catholics who had
stored arms for the defense of the Church of St. Philip
of Neri.

Thus even the various investigating bodies proved to
be anti-Catholic, though varying in directly naming the
Catholics as responsible for the May and July riots.

The 1844 riots shocked fair-minded Americans, and
most Protestants were repelled by the lawlessness of the
Philadelphia mobs. However, the bitterness against the
Irish Catholics erupted in riots in other cities during the
1840s and continued under the Know-Nothing movement
of the 1850s, with its "American" views. Religious prejudice dies slowly.

ASTOR PLACE RIOT
New York City
May 10, 1849

The Fight Against
the Feuding Foreigner

THE Native American movement was based upon the dislike of anything or anyone foreign. But since the largest number of immigrants were from Great Britain (which included Ireland at the time), they were the chief targets of "American" wrath. The hatred of the Irish took the form of anti-Catholicism (see Chapter 4), but the English presented a difficult problem, partly because so many "Americans" were of direct British lineage. In a sense the British were rivals, and therefore the belittling of Englishmen was more personal than general.

The British, on the other hand, felt themselves superior in every way to the descendants of their former colonists. England had a centuries-old and revered history, while the United States was an infant in the family of nations. Travelers from Europe—authors, lecturers, and the merely curious—took great pleasure in visiting our country and deriding it afterward. Charles Dickens, for example, wrote his highly critical *American Notes* after a visit in 1842, calling the United States "a cultural wasteland."

The Americans had not forgotten the bitterness of the War of 1812. By the middle of the nineteenth century the mutual feeling was antagonism.

In the early half of the last century the best actors of both England and the United States toured each country regularly. They often played the same roles, particularly Shakespearean.

A feud that was followed avidly and even encouraged by the newspapers began in 1844 between William Macready, a well-known and eminent English tragedian, and Edwin Forrest, an equally noted American actor. Both played the same roles and enjoyed the admiration of faithful followers (who would today be called "fans"). Both were somewhat spoiled by the adulation and praise they received.

Macready had the misfortune to be English at a time when Nativism was at its height in our country. He had become acquainted with all parts of the United States (at that time east of the Mississippi River), understood and admired the American spirit, and was even intending to retire in Cambridge, Massachusetts, after his last tour in 1848-49. He began to sense the hostility of some of his audiences in 1844; there were occasional hisses and catcalls amidst the usual thunderous applause. The press began to imply that these "groaners," as they were called, were supporters of Edwin Forrest.

Macready's loyal followers and the English critics returned the inhospitality when Forrest made his next tour of Britain. Both actors were quite voluble in belittling each other's abilities. The press and public enjoyed the feud, and the critics, who were supposed to be fair-minded, wrote biased reviews. The quarrel between the two men became intensely personal when Macready, in a performance of *Hamlet* in Edinburgh in 1846, was hissed by Forrest, who was in a side-stage box. Macready had substituted some of his own gestures for the traditional ones, and a fellow actor described the sound as "a long, sustained hiss, like the sound of a steam engine." Forrest was readily recognized, and several days later talked and laughed through Macready's main scene. The resulting uproar made the conflict bitter and Forrest's American admirers began to capitalize on the fact that Macready was English.

When the British actor began his pre-retirement American tour in the fall of 1848, he was received by a hostile press and his performances were frequently interrupted by noisy members of the audience. During a Philadelphia performance of *Macbeth* in October a section of the audience hissed him continuously, and in the fifth act a rotten egg was smashed on the stage. At the final curtain applause was mixed with booing, and Macready, in a curtain speech, referred to his impolite and ungracious treatment by "an American actor."

In May 1849 Forrest unwisely attacked his English enemy in a long "card" (which nowadays would be a paid advertisement) in the leading Philadelphia paper. In this he cited the "insults he had suffered"; his accusations were nearly libelous, since the attack called Macready many offensive names. The Briton stoutly defended himself, and the fat was in the fire. At all stops on his tour through the South to New Orleans and back to New York by way of Cincinnati, he discovered that the Native Americans were united in persecuting him.

In what was something more than mere coincidence, both Forrest and Macready were scheduled to play *Macbeth* on Monday, May 7, 1849, the latter's opening night in New York, where Forrest was performing his varied repertoire at the Broadway Theater (Macready played only Shakespearean roles). The newspapers lost no time in capitalizing on "the great theatrical warfare," for the "theatrical excitement has been rising to fever heat."

The Astor Place Opera House, the latter term used interchangeably with "Theater," where Macready was to appear, was a new and imposing colonnaded building fronting Lafayette Place and the Bowery on the east and the present Eighth Street on the north. The main entrance was on Astor Place, to the south. The large theater seated eighteen hundred.

Because of the rumors of trouble, a few police were stationed outside the theater. The house was sold out and the audience was a mixture of the aristocratic and the common. All went well until the entrance of Macready. Before he could speak the first line, a rotten egg whistled just past his head and a man shouted, "Down with the English hog!" For fifteen minutes the star waited for the turmoil to cease, then finally began the scene. *Macbeth* continued, but it was completely inaudible. A flurry of copper pennies pelted from above tinkled on the stage, and within minutes the players were dodging a rain of apples, lemons, potatoes, and bits of wood. A bottle of asafetida splashed on Macready. The uproar continued to the beginning of the third act. A shower of chairs finally forced an early end to the performance.

Macready was inclined to cancel the rest of his scheduled performances, but an open letter signed by forty-eight leading citizens reassured him that the "lawlessness did not speak for America" and urged him to "grant the city an opportunity to wipe out the disgrace inflicted upon its character." He accordingly agreed to perform again on Thursday evening, May 10. Forrest changed his schedule so that he would also play *Macbeth* on that night, and the announcements were posted next to each other.

At the same time a handbill was displayed throughout the city, reading: "Workingmen! Shall Americans or Englishmen rule in this country? The crews of the British steamers have threatened all Americans who shall dare to appear this night at the Opera House. Workingmen! Freemen! Stand up to your lawful rights!" This was an obvious warning of impending violence, and the chief of police promised a large force to preserve order, while two regiments of the city militia were placed on a stand-by alert. To keep out the Nativist adherents of Forrest, tickets were sold only to those known to be in sympathy with Macready. A ticket seller later recalled, however, that an unusual number of purchasers "spoke with aristocratic English accents." These were actors hired by Ned Buntline, an avid Nativist and advocate of "America for Americans," to purchase tickets in adjoining rows.

Astor Place was crowded long before curtain time. Three hundred police had been assigned, two hundred inside to preserve order, the remainder posted in groups

around it. The famous Seventh Infantry Regiment under
the command of General Sandford had been able to
gather about two hundred of their number at its downtown headquarters. Two troops each of cavalry and light
artillery, the latter supplied with two cannons, waited
in readiness.

The apparently peaceful audience was composed almost entirely of men, with only about half a dozen
women. Police were stationed everywhere—on the sides,
on stairways, at the foot of the aisles, and in the balcony
and gallery. The curtain rose ten minutes late, at seven-
forty. When Macready made his first appearance a storm
of cheers, groans, and hisses broke loose. Nine tenths of
the audience was friendly, and to show their support gave
him a fifteen-minute ovation, applauding, cheering, and
waving hats and handkerchiefs, while the far outnumbered anti-Macready forces created an even greater
racket, shouting and shaking their fists. The play resumed
only after a placard bearing the notice, "The friends of
order will remain silent," was pushed out from the wings.
But most of the dialogue could not be heard because of
the continued hissing and booing from groups seated together in the orchestra and the gallery. The police finally
marched down the aisles. Four of the ringleaders were
arrested and detained in the basement beneath the orchestra, while the others were thrown out into the street.

When they joined their comrades there the time was
ripe for an attack. Unfortunately, a sewer was under construction and loose paving stones lay in neat piles on the
curb. At once many of the theater windows on Eighth
Street, which had been covered by nailing planks across

them, were shattered; the barrage of the stones and pieces from a nearby marbleyard cracked the boards and they gave way. Stones fell inside the theater and some of the patrons in the orchestra left their seats to seek the protection of the balcony. At the same time smoke began seeping through the floor; the arrested ringleaders had started a fire which soon petered out. The din continued as the crowd outside battered on the barred doors, hoping to force them open.

Outside the theater the crowd "was wild with excitement," and at the main entrance "were wrought up to the highest pitch, heaving to and fro like the waves of the ocean." Witnesses later estimated the number to be from ten to twenty thousand. The police were unable to bring such a mob under control, even when they moved in a solid mass in vain attempts to disperse the crowd. Attacked with stones and missiles and pressed upon by cursing citizens, a good many of whom were riffraff from downtown, these police could barely defend themselves and were in danger of being surrounded and trapped. Several lay bleeding on the pavement, praying that they might be spared by the mob.

Realizing that this was no momentary disturbance and that a full-scale riot of the most terrifying type was in the making, the sheriff ordered the police to move inside the theater and sent for the waiting military forces. The first to arrive was a troop of cavalry. They had barely galloped into sight before stones and brickbats unhorsed several. The mounts became so restive and unmanageable that the others fled the scene. It was now nine o'clock and the third act of the play continued.

During the fourth act a stone hit the chandelier and a shower of glass fragments scattered the few of the audience still seated in the orchestra. But Macready and his cast completed the drama, and a short time later he joined a few stragglers in the audience and reached his hotel without being detected. This was his last performance in America, for he was smuggled out of New York the next day and sailed from Boston a fortnight later, never to return.

Meanwhile, the small body of infantry marched into a huge wedge of rioters. The street lights had been shot out and in the semidarkness of the clouded moon all was confusion. The crowd bore down ever more heavily, but the well-disciplined soldiers forced their way through the mob and were able to clear Eighth Street, not, however, without some injuries. A cordon of police was set up to seal off the street. At this time the play ended and the audience left the theater.

The main body of soldiers, now reduced by casualties to only seventy, swung around the theater to face the huge crowd on Astor Place, intending to force it back there. The rioters retreated at the sight of the bayoneted muskets, but when the advancing soldiers reached the center of the opera house, the mob could move no farther because of the press of the thickly packed crowd in the square. They turned on their aggressors and, evidently doubting that the soldiers would fire, fearlessly pelted them with stones and sharp-edged bricks (the supply was apparently inexhaustible). Some of the more daring struggled with soldiers, seizing their guns, forty in all.

At this critical moment a pistol shot fired from the

crowd struck one of the captains. The general in command shouted above the din, ordering the rioters to fall back and disperse or they would be fired upon. The answer was even louder hooting and booing and a concerted rush during which the general and several soldiers in the front rank were knocked down. The force was pushed back toward the opera house in continuous showers of stones.

The general then gave the order to charge with bayonets, but the crowd was so close that this was impossible. Again his repeated warnings were received with defiant shouts of "Fire, if you dare!" Only those closest could hear above the pandemonium. The colonel gave the order to fire over the heads of the crowd, to aim at a wall opposite. Instead of being intimidated the mob seemed to take renewed courage, renewing their taunts and mockery. "They have only blank cartridges! Give it to them again!" and another volley of paving stones followed, this time with telling effect. Muskets were again wrenched from the soldiers' hands, and "stones as large as your double fist were pelted like a shower of hail."

Now the colonel ordered the soldiers, "Fire low!" They did, and several men fell. For a moment the astonished mob halted in disbelief while the dead and wounded were carried off. Then they renewed the attack but were driven away. Undaunted, they rallied in two sections and again advanced. This time the order was "Fire obliquely!" and the soldiers obeyed, one half shooting to the right, the other half to the left. Three successive volleys were fired into the swaying mob, each taking its toll in casualties and bloodshed. These were the final shots. The crowd began falling back, still, however, bombarding the soldiers with missiles.

A small space was finally cleared in front of the theater and two brass cannons loaded with grapeshot were hauled up and pointed to command the two main streets. Under this sobering demonstration of forceful intentions the crowd broke up into small groups and finally only a few citizens remained in the area, tending to the wounded and carrying them to a nearby drugstore to which the casualties had been taken throughout the evening. The dead were soon taken away. The wounded soldiers (by some good fortune none were killed) were treated in the halls of the theater.

The most reliable estimate of casualties was 31 killed and 150 wounded. Some were merely spectators who had taken no part in the riot, or citizens who were passing at the time.

The news of the affair caused a great stir in the city. The thwarted rioters called a protest meeting to be held in City Hall Park at six o'clock on Friday, the day after the riot. "The sacrifice of human lives in the vicinity of the Astor Place Opera House last night was the most wanton, unprovoked, and murderous outrage ever perpetrated in the civilized world," stated the resulting resolution. The police and military were censured for their "barbarous treatment of peace-loving citizens," and a full inquiry was called for.

A complete investigation of the riot was undertaken by the coroner's jury, which found that "the persons killed came to their death from gunshot wounds fired by the military, by order of the civil authorities," and that "the circumstances that existed at the time justified the authorities in giving orders to fire upon the mob."

Eighty-six rioters had been arrested and held overnight in the basement of the theater; sixty-five were held for trial, but only ten were finally tried in September, for specific evidence was difficult to obtain. All were found guilty and sentenced to prison terms ranging from one month to one year.

In his charge to the jury Judge Charles P. Daly said that the members were to determine whether or not there was evidence of conspiracy and/or riot. His definition of "riot" became the generally accepted one thereafter (see Chapter 1).

Before the Astor Place Riot it was the legal opinion that no one could be prosecuted for a riot, as it was presumed to be "the natural effect of political passion." Judge Daly's charge completely reversed this concept, and prosecution for rioting became accepted under American law.

DRAFT RIOT
New York City
July 13-16, 1863

"A Rich Man's War, A Poor Man's Fight"

THE United States was in the throes of a tragic division in 1863. When the Southern states seceded from the Union in the spring of 1861, the Northerners had felt certain that their industrial superiority would make the war short. But the Confederacy proved to be a stubborn, dedicated, and unyielding foe. At the beginning of 1863 the Union Army needed more men than the volunteer system could supply.

After heated discussion the United States Congress passed the National Conscription Act, which was signed by President Lincoln on March 3. This legislation was the first in which the federal government sought to create a citizen army without the aid of state authorities, and the first to fix the principle that every able-bodied male citizen had an obligation to perform military service. Men between the ages of twenty and forty-five were to be enrolled, and if their names were drawn they would serve for three years.

An objectionable and troublemaking feature of the Act was the provision that anyone whose name was drawn could pay three hundred dollars to the local draft board for a substitute or furnish his own acceptable replacement. This obviously favored the rich, for the weekly wage of the average laborer was twenty dollars.

The Act had established a quota of 300,000; New York City's was 33,000. The enrollment, in a house-to-house canvass, was completed on June 29, and the drawings were set to begin on Saturday, July 11, 1863. This interval unfortunately permitted the development of vigorous opposition among the poor of the city, particularly the Irish, who formed a quarter of the 800,000 population. About ten per cent of the city's foreign-born were known criminals. The poor thoroughly resented the exemption clause, voicing their disapproval with the cry, "A rich man's war, a poor man's fight!"

New York City had been divided into congressional districts, six in Manhattan, each under the supervision of a provost marshal, with a civilian draft board and a doctor. The eligibles were not given draft cards, as in the World War I draft and subsequent years. Their names, written on slips of paper, were placed in a revolving wooden box or lottery wheel, from which the quota number would be drawn by a civilian.

The initial drawing in the Ninth District office at Third Avenue and Forty-sixth Street took place on Saturday, the eleventh, and seven hundred names were read off without incident. But opponents—war-weary Democrats, Southern sympathizers, and Confederate agitators—were active on Sunday. By Monday morning they had set the stage for what were to become the longest, most wide-spread, and most destructive riots in American history, with by far the largest number of rioters.

The four-day New York City Draft Riots were unique in several features. The participants totaled seventy thousand, swarming through the streets at times in screaming, frenzied herds of ten thousand. Since the police force amounted to a little over two thousand, they were often outnumbered by five hundred to one. The riotous mobs did not limit their ravages to a single neighborhood or area, as is usual in riots, but instead covered all parts of the city from downtown Manhattan to Harlem, and on both the east and west sides of the Fifth Avenue dividing line in what is now midtown.

Nor were the riots confined to a single day, or even the daylight hours; four days and nights, even until the early morning, the crowds roamed the city without pause in a continuous orgy of destruction. They committed every sort of crime—murder, lynching, looting, and burning. One of the city's newspapers correctly called the riots "a carnival of violence."

The riots started as a treasonable insurrection against the United States Government, then became a destructive attack against the well-to-do, and finally a race riot with Negroes as targets. Scores of separate incidents were equal in fury to many full-scale riots.

The New York City Draft Riots offer the best single example of a mob expanding its original objective to anarchy and every sort of crime and violence.

Seldom has a mob taken over a metropolis and terrified its citizens so completely before being subdued by artillery and musket fire. The range of mob activities was so vast and the countless individual outbursts of such savage fury and appalling destruction that only a few of the highlights can be mentioned within this chapter.

Early in the morning of Monday, July 13, 1863, small groups of workingmen began to assemble as if by pre-arrangement on the street corners of the western industrial section of the city below Fifty-ninth Street. As they moved toward Central Park their number and strength increased at every factory they passed. Leaders harangued them in the park, fixing the Third Avenue draft office as their objective.

The crowd accordingly moved down Fifth Avenue, four thousand strong. Some carried signs bearing the words "Down with the Draft" and "No Draft." Other crowds had already broken into a hardware store near the office and armed themselves with axes with which they tore down the wires of the police telegraph system to stop any possible interference. They barricaded the street with the poles. A crowd packed the street solidly for twelve blocks, waiting for the fun to begin.

At the appointed hour of 10 A.M. the front doors of the draft office were opened and those nearest the door poured in. The regular turns of the wheel had produced about a hundred names, each called out, when suddenly a large paving block came crashing through the window, followed immediately by a pistol shot and a shower of stones and bricks.

The time was ten thirty-five. The riot had begun.

The mob rushed the door, overwhelming the police guard. The draft wheel was destroyed and all the records were torn to bits. Someone spread turpentine on the floor and set the office ablaze. Soon dense smoke began to pour into the street, and some of the cheering crowd beat the firemen off when they attempted to attach the hoses to the hydrants. Within an hour the entire block from Forty-sixth to Forty-seventh streets was in flames.

John Kennedy, the superintendent of police, approached the spot in civilian clothes but was recognized and beaten into insensibility before being rescued. Meanwhile arriving police detachments, outnumbered two hundred to one, were overwhelmed by the savage mob and escaped only by a miracle. A unit of locally stationed federal soldiers armed with sabers and muskets was met by a shower of paving stones and brickbats; one was killed and six wounded within five minutes. The troops opened fire, killing seven rioters but only momentarily checking the mob, who attacked again and again. Only a few soldiers were able to escape without being severely beaten.

The draft machinery had been destroyed, but the mob's fury was undiminished. Part of the crowd surged south on Third Avenue. Their target was the building on Second Avenue and Twenty-first Street housing a huge gun factory with a state armory on the fifth floor. Police armed with night sticks, revolvers, and carbines had already taken their positions at the doors and windows. About ten thousand men and women were soon packed in the surrounding streets, hurling bricks and paving stones, firing pistols and muskets.

Led by a giant thug waving a sledge hammer, a group attempted to force the entrance door and managed to smash in a panel. The first to crawl through was killed instantly. The sight of his headless and bloody body served to renew the mob's rage. They came on again with sledges and crowbars, and formed human battering rams with telephone poles. The police inside escaped through a rear smoke exhaust pipe.

When the doors gave way the rioters swarmed on the various floors, a few making their way to the top-floor drill room to seize the precious carbines and ammunition stored there. They barricaded the door so that they would not be discovered. From every window of the factory carbines were thrown to those waiting below. Others formed a human chain along which the guns were passed out to the street.

Police officers using their clubs freely were finally able to clear a path to the doorway. Fearing that those inside would be arrested, some rioters set fire to the building in a dozen places. The flames spread rapidly, and those on the first floor were clubbed unmercifully by the waiting police as they tried to escape. The looters on the fifth floor found themselves trapped by the flames when they opened the barricaded door. Some leaped to their deaths from the windows. Many more were killed in the roaring inferno when the floor collapsed at about 4:30 P.M. The dead were never counted, for only bones and ashes were later found. In the entire four-hour attack, twenty-five rioters were known to have been killed and more than seventy-five seriously wounded. Two thousand finished carbines had been stolen and were to be put to good use.

Meanwhile, the second group of several hundred from the Third Avenue draft office fire started west across town. En route they passed through a district of new and elegant brownstone houses. Here lived the rich who could afford to buy their way out of the draft. Scores of mansions were attacked and looted from cellar to roof, with fine furniture, mirrors, and china smashed or thrown from the windows. About a thousand continued to Fifth Avenue, stopping en route to drink up the liquor in a bar.

On Fifth Avenue between Forty-third and Forty-fourth streets was located the Colored Orphan Asylum, which housed about two hundred and fifty children below the age of twelve. The building reminded the now befuddled mob of the hated draft. The war, they had been told, was being fought to free the slaves. These Negroes were responsible! The superintendent was given five minutes to remove the children, while a crowd swarmed on the front lawn and stormed to the doors, starting to batter them in. After systematically pillaging every room in the large four-story building, the asylum was set afire. By six o'clock only smoking ashes remained, for the crowd had cut the hoses of the arriving fire companies.

Another group had meanwhile attacked the draft office of the Eighth District at Broadway and Twenty-eighth Street and both looted and burned the entire block in which it was located. Still another crowd marched down Fifth Avenue and were prevented from attacking the mayor's house by a strong police guard. Thus frustrated, they marched farther downtown, intending to loot the banks in the financial district. But a crack squad of the police dispersed them after a half-hour pitched battle with many cracked heads. Later in the evening a mob attacked the office of the *Tribune*, seeking Horace Greeley, its pro-war editor. They set the building afire, but the blaze was extinguished and the police again scattered them.

The race riot within this many-faceted riot began in the afternoon. Negroes on the street were attacked and beaten soundly, on the pretext that they were responsible for the war, hence the draft. While the *Tribune* was being assaulted a large mob visited a nearby Negro section, throwing furniture into the street and burning it and, finally, an entire block of rickety houses. Every colored person attempting to escape was punished by a beating.

The first Negro lynching occurred early on Monday evening. Several hundred men and boys seized a helpless colored man, beat him into insensibility, hanged him by a rope thrown over the limb of a tree, hacked his body, and finally built a fire to roast the corpse. A few hours later a Negro mother was beaten to death while attempting to protect her crippled son.

The hard-pressed police had done valiant work, but they needed help badly, and nearly a thousand citizen police were rapidly sworn in. By Tuesday morning state militiamen were being mobilized and the mayor had asked that federal troops be sent to the city from Gettysburg. "The situation," he said, "is desperate." It was indeed.

By a strange coincidence, Tuesday, July 14, was the seventy-fourth anniversary of the fall of the Bastille, which marked the beginning of the French Revolution with a mob in control of the city of Paris. In New York City the anti-law rabble were well on the way to taking over the metropolis completely.

The day began with the early morning murders of two

Negroes. The houses of the colored people throughout the city were almost systematically plundered and burned and three more victims were murdered after dark.

The soldiers first met the mob with sabers, muskets, and cannons during the morning at Second Avenue and Thirty-fourth Street. At its peak the crowd there numbered ten thousand. The police and soldiers walked into a cunning trap. Thousands of bricks were thrown from the rooftops and the street mobs held their own until the firing of cannons directly into the closely packed crowd was effective in clearing the area. In the afternoon other mobs captured the Union Steam Works, a munitions factory, but before the contents could be removed, these rioters were cleared out by hand-to-hand, inch-by-inch fighting with the police in an hour-long battle.

Roving gangs covered every section of the city while the major outbreaks were taking place. The day was one of great robberies. Hundreds of stores, including the famous Brooks Brothers, were looted. The deserted homes of the wealthy were plundered and, in some cases, burned.

The peak of the mob violence in the afternoon was on the west side near Ninth Avenue and Forty-second Street. Throngs of rioters hacked down telegraph poles and lampposts to barricade the streets, reinforcing them with carts, furniture, barrels, and boxes piled high. The combined forces of the police and militia fought from block to block, forcing the protected defenders to retreat, leaving the dead and the wounded at the barricades.

Tuesday had proved to be the height of the violence, but the uprising was far from finished. Governor Seymour of New York belatedly issued a proclamation declaring the city to be in a state of insurrection. But five regiments of troops were en route, and the reign of the rabble would inevitably be finished.

The orgy of murder and pillage continued on Wednesday. Three more Negroes were lynched, many were beaten and their tenement homes sacked and burned. A reporter characterized the chase thus: "It was a case of the hares and the hounds."

The lawless crowds now lacked any direction. They had failed to obtain arms in sufficient quantity to overcome the rapidly increasing forces of law and order. They had suffered large numbers of casualties and their original purpose had long since been forgotten. The violence continued only because of the momentum which had been built up. Wednesday night would mark the end of mob rule.

From four o'clock until after midnight the east side was the scene of the last desperate mob outbreaks. The streets became battlegrounds as newly arrived units of soldiers set up howitzers and fired time and time again into the assembled crowds, meanwhile advancing in solid ranks. Scores of rioters manned the rooftops, firing muskets and pistols and pelting the soldiers with bricks and missiles. The battle raged incessantly, the ever increasing rashness and desperation of the mob being met by active displays of force. Howitzers continually raked the streets, but toward midnight quiet was restored, though pillaging of stores and shops continued until dawn.

Fresh federal troops poured into the beleaguered city on Thursday, and the constant patrols prevented the formation of mobs. The few last-ditch pockets of resistance were successfully broken up. The riots were over.

The weary police and soldiers began attempting to recover the stolen loot. Damage claims amounting to two million dollars (the present-day equivalent of ten million) were paid from a Riot Damage Indemnity Fund raised by bond issues. Business loss was incalculable.

The most quoted figure of killed was one thousand, but a maximum of five hundred seems more nearly accurate. The number of seriously wounded was reliably stated at nearly a thousand. More than four hundred police and three hundred militiamen and soldiers suffered serious injury.

Whatever the correct figures may have been, the days of the Draft Riots were aptly termed "the bloody week." Since their essential purpose was to "rise up against civil or political authority," they were also an insurrection.

Because the police were completely occupied in subduing the outbreaks throughout the city, few arrests were made. Of 198 citizens indicted by a grand jury, only 89 were brought to trial, and only 55 received sentences. The Democratic judges, obviously sympathetic to the objectives of the disorders, either dismissed cases or imposed minimum sentences.

The government never even considered abolishing the draft in New York City, and the clause permitting payment for a substitute remained in effect. The enrollment records of the two burned district offices had been saved, and the drawings resumed on August 25 under the protection of federal soldiers who had remained in the city.

The July terror in New York City has been termed by one of its historians "the largest violent, most brutal outbreak in our country's history."

ANTI-CHINESE RIOT
Los Angeles
October 24, 1871

Massacre in the Calle de los Negros

FOLLOWING the gold discoveries of 1848 in California, because of the shortage of labor in the boom period, the Chinese were welcomed on the Pacific coast, particularly as house servants, cooks, gardeners, and laundrymen. Then, because Chinese native labor was cheap, six companies under contract imported shiploads of indentured coolies, paying for their passage and assigning them on arrival to mining or railroad companies. This influx formed the basis of ever growing racial prejudice, because their presence reduced the wages of all laborers, including whites, while increasing the profits of the owners.

Public resentment of the Chinese in California began in the mid-1860s, when Pacific Coast residents began openly to express fear of the Orientals, characterizing them as "the Chinese menace." In 1870 the actual number of Chinese in the United States was only 62,000, since more than half the imported coolies had by then returned to their homeland. The Burlingame Treaty with

China in 1868 confirmed the right of the Chinese to expatriate themselves without the necessity of becoming American citizens.

In 1871 Los Angeles, the City of the Angels, was a small, rambling town of only 6,000 population. The buildings of wood and adobe were reminders of the days of the Spaniards, and the streets bore Spanish names. A section of "downtown," near Calle Principal (Main Street) formed the segregated area where most of the Chinese and Mexicans lived peaceably together. This area near the plaza, the cathedral, and present-day Olvera Street bordered on the Calle de los Negros, locally translated as Negro or Black Alley, which was the center of the local underworld and its attendant gambling, drinking, roistering, and crime.

The small Chinese community lived mainly in the Coronel Block, an L-shaped building with a long raised porch on all sides, including the interior corral. The apartments were almost all connected by doors.

Following the customs of their native land, the Chinese of the town formed associations or companies called "tongs," all being rivals of one another. On Friday evening, October 20, a civil ceremony of marriage, very unusual at the time, was performed by a justice of the peace for a young man, Ah Choy, of the Nin Yung group and his bride, who belonged to (was literally owned by) the rival Hong Chow Company. The purpose of the civil ceremony was apparently to avoid payment for the bride, since female ownership was then the accepted rule. Tong warfare resulted.

Four days later, on Tuesday, October 24, the first

skirmish between members of the Nin Yung and Hong Chow companies took place in Negro Alley, when two members exchanged pistol shots—without injuries, however. When both were arrested and booked for attempted murder, a Nin Yung merchant, Sam Yuen, bailed out Ah Choy, his clansman, with six thousand dollars in gold which he claimed to have in his store. When a police officer corroborated this story by actually seeing the cache, Ah Choy was set free. The fact that a Chinese held such wealth on his premises was not overlooked as a topic of conversation in barrooms and bordellos, and was to play a role in the looting which was a part of the massacre later in the day.

At that time the Los Angeles police force numbered six men, and Chief (Marshal) Francis Baker, feeling that the fighting was not over, assigned mounted officer Jesus Bilderrain to patrol the area just as Ah Choy returned. All was apparently peaceful. But no sooner had he finished his rounds than shots rang out from Negro Alley. The tongs were again settling their differences, and this time the bridegroom Ah Choy had received a wound which was to prove fatal three days later.

Officer Bilderrain asked an armed bystander to help him catch the fleeing Chinese, but they were fired upon from inside the Coronel Block. Bilderrain entered the house but soon staggered out, without his pistol and with a gunshot wound on his shoulder. He blew a long blast on his police whistle. A rancher named Robert Thompson and a fellow policeman appeared and were soon pouring pistol shots into the houses in the block. Since these were not returned, Thompson fearlessly yet foolhardily approached a door. He was met by a barrage of shots from the inside of the house and staggered backward with a bullet in his chest, dying an hour later.

At that moment Marshal Baker arrived and deputized guards from the crowd that had assembled. He then ordered them to surround the entire block and shoot any Chinese who might try to escape. Some of them went to the corral at the back of the block and were greeted by gunfire from fleeing Chinese. A group of men had meanwhile seized Wong Tuck, an armed resident of a house across from the Coronel Block, and were obviously planning to lynch him when a peace officer released him and permitted him to return to his house amid shots fired by members of the crowd.

No further efforts were made to locate those who had shot Bilderrain and Thompson. But the news had spread quickly and attracted a crowd which grew more restive by the minute. When Robert Thompson died in a drugstore two blocks away at approximately six o'clock, less than two hours after he had been shot, the news transformed the uneasy crowd in Negro Alley into an unreasoning mob. The story was elaborated upon elsewhere throughout the town (in this case the usual false report that often triggers a riot) to the effect that the Chinese were "killing whites wholesale!"

The head of the town's single volunteer fire company, organized only a month before, arrived at the scene and was prevailed upon to let the fire hose be used in an attempt to flush out the entrapped Chinese. The Chicago fire had occurred only two weeks before, he later said in justification of his action, and he felt that it would be wise to be prepared should anyone in the mob decide to fire the building in which the Chinese were penned. But this attempt to force them out proved a failure and was abandoned.

The death of Thompson had fired the crowd to fever pitch and its anger needed a target. The once captured and once released Wong Tuck at this moment made another try to get away from his house, this time armed with a hatchet. Immediately on his appearance he was seized, but released to two peace officers who started to walk with him to the jail four blocks away. The eager crowd churned around them, shouting for Tuck's life. The officers were attacked and Wong Tuck was taken by the mob. A rope appeared as if by magic and within minutes the unlucky Chinese was dangling from the gate of the Tomlinson Corral, a lumberyard nearby. While most of the crowd returned to the alley, a few lingered to amuse themselves by banging the dead man's head back and forth against one of the gate's uprights until it was a bloody pulpy mass.

By now the crowd in Negro Alley had greatly increased: a mixture of the merely curious peaceable citizens and the more numerous trigger-happy riffraff who always gather and assume command when crowds show signs of resorting to violence. This element was composed of scores of ruffians, thieves, gamblers, thugs, and idlers who found the lax local law enforcement to their taste.

In the common pattern of riots, such a restless crowd responds to the harangues of a self-appointed leader, and now a fiery-tongued orator made inflammatory anti-Chinese speeches. When a police officer was bold enough to attempt to silence him the crowd became threatening, and the tirades continued. The Coronel Block was still under strong guard of the citizen deputies.

Concerted mob action began in the darkness shortly after nine o'clock. Since the earlier fire hose tactic had been unsuccessful, another maneuver was tried. Some men climbed up on the flat roof of the Coronel Block and with pickaxes chopped holes through it, then poured gunfire into the apartments below. The result was immediate. Two Chinese ran into the street, meeting the fatal gunfire of the crowd. The crowd's score was now three dead, and the bodies of these two victims were strung up from a porch.

Since continued gunfire through the roof failed to flush out more victims, some of the restless crowd devised other methods. "Get the Chinks out!" shouted those who were waiting.

Some hoodlums found a large rock that had fallen off a wagon earlier in the day and used it as a battering ram to break in the doors. But they were afraid to follow up this action by entering. The Chinese inside made neither a move nor a sound.

"Burn the Chinks!" now became the cry. An ingenious inventor produced a kind of fireball and threw it through the opening made by the rock. A police officer ordered him to retrieve it and, when he flatly refused to enter alone, went inside with him. They soon threw the fireball out into the middle of Negro Alley, where for a long time it gave light for the climactic events of the riot.

Since the two came out without incident, the crowd assumed it was now safe to enter the building, and they eagerly poured through the doorways, finding dozens of men and women attempting to hide in their apartments. Two or three already killed by the gunfire through the roof were thrown out into the streets, where their bodies were beaten and kicked before being dragged off to be hanged. Rings were torn from their fingers and in several instances, if a ring proved too tight, a finger was chopped off.

Of the Chinese found alive, some were dragged along the street to various hanging places. A large number of citizens and deputy guards, unnoticed in the confusion, were meanwhile able to rescue many men, women, and children and take them to the safety of the jail. A policeman—the one who had been shown the cache of gold in Sam Yuen's store—figured that the time was favorable for a bit of private enterprise and began to make his way to the premises. En route he seized several Chinese and turned them over to the mob, directing the custodians to take them to the safety of the jail. Instead they were doomed to the gallows. One of the victims was shot through the mouth and robbed before being strung up.

The porch roof of Goller's wagon shop, a block from Negro Alley, became the busiest gallows. The ropes were clotheslines given the crowd by the proprietress of a boardinghouse. Six bodies finally swung from the roof truss.

At the same time other rioters were hanging Chinese from the sides of two prairie schooners that were standing nearby, still others from the crossbeam of the gate of the Tomlinson Corral where Wong Tuck had been the first to be hanged. The gate was guarded by men with loaded rifles and pistols aimed at the crowd in case some citizens should attempt to interfere. Five victims, including a fourteen-year-old boy, were hanged simultaneously, the five ropes pulled by honored ruffians selected from the mob. All those hanged had previously been shot, stabbed, or beaten, and blood, rare in ordinary hangings, was spattered everywhere.

While these four hanging parties were venting their fury on their captives, scores of the mob members were systematically pillaging the vacated quarters, seizing anything of value available. The looting continued throughout the night without interference. No peace officer or citizen was willing to risk his life by intervening. The situation was completely without remedy, and the law enforcement officers failed even to summon the federal troops stationed at Drum Barracks in Wilmington, only twenty miles away by railroad.

Meanwhile law-abiding citizens could only hide their Chinese servants and cooks from the possible rage of the lawless mob. By eleven o'clock on the evening of October 24, 1871, the mob had completed its acts of vengeance and eighteen mutilated bodies were swaying at ropes' ends—six at the wagon shop, five at the Tomlinson Corral, four at the Coronel Block, and three from the freight prairie schooners. The body of the first victim, Wong Tuck, had been cut down at the Tomlinson Corral and dragged to a cemetery. When Ah Choy, the wounded bridegroom, died three days later, the total became twenty, though some writers raise the total to twenty-two or twenty-three.

The number shot (but not subsequently hanged) was

never revealed, for a veil of discreet silence was drawn over printed reports and later trial testimony. The lack of information was undoubtedly due to the fact that the mob, at its largest numbering about six hundred, a tenth of the population, included many prominent citizens who succumbed to their anti-Chinese prejudices under the stimulus of the riotous crowd. Some of these became leaders in the city's later development.

In addition to the slaughter, the Chinese quarters were looted of more than thirty thousand dollars in money and personal property. This included the six thousand dollars in gold hidden in Sam Yuen's store. When he sued the town of Los Angeles for this loss on the basis of negligence of the public protective forces, the all-white jury made no award. Sam Yuen, they stated, had failed to take "reasonable diligence" by notifying the sheriff or mayor that a riot was in the making on that October afternoon!

A special grand jury was convened a week later. The number of indictments for murder, never made public, was variously reported as thirty, thirty-nine, and a hundred and fifty. Only ten participants were brought to trial on March 17, 1872, and they were charged with the murder of Doctor Chin Lee Tong, one of the victims. After abundant private testimony, eight were pronounced guilty and two not guilty. They were given sentences varying from two to six years each, to be served at San Quentin state prison. Scores of those indicted, however, were never brought to trial. Everyone agreed unanimously that the "regrettable" incident should be forgotten.

A little more than a year later the California Supreme

Court reversed the Los Angeles jury's verdict. "The indictment in this case is fatally defective in that it fails to
allege that Chin Lee Tong was murdered," the statement
read. "It is alleged that the defendants did stand by, aid,
abet, assist, advise, counsel and encourage one John Doe
and one Richard Roe to feloniously, unlawfully, willfully,
deliberately, premeditatedly and of their malice afore-
thought, to kill and murder one Chin Lee Tong," the
astounding legal opinion continued. "Admitting that the
defendants did all these things, still it does not follow
by necessary legal conclusions that, after all, any person
was actually murdered." The prison doors were opened,
and all could breathe a sigh of relief, for "justice" had
been done. The defendants were never reindicted.

The "China riot" became a matter of history. But the
"Chinese problem" remained and the blind racism which
punished the entire Chinese community of Los Angeles
for the murder of a single white man persisted. San
Francisco's Sand Lots riot in 1877 was triggered when
Dennis Kearney harangued unemployed workmen with
the cry "The Chinese must go!" because imported coolies
were working for the Central Pacific Railway for sixty-
five cents a day. The property of many Chinese was
sacked and burned. Other major anti-Chinese riots occurred in Denver in 1880 and in a Rock Springs, Wyo-
ming, mining camp in 1885.

The hue and cry against Orientals (including also the
Japanese) resulted in enactment of the Exclusion Acts of
1882 and 1892, applying particularly to the importation
of laborers and making the Chinese ineligible for citizen-
ship (a voiding of the 1868 Burlingame Treaty). The

Immigration Act of 1924 prohibited the entrance of all Asiatic laborers.

All these discriminatory laws were repealed by the U. S. Congress in 1943, and since then Chinese immigration has been regulated under a quota system.

As the years have passed, anti-Chinese prejudice has disappeared. In the cities with large Chinese populations living together according to their preference in "Chinatowns," police officials report the rate of crime in those areas to be low and criminal acts practically non-existent. Their sense of family closeness and veneration of the elders is enviable. They have earned the respect of the communities where they live.

STEEL LOCKOUT
Homestead, Pa.
July 1892

The Bloodiest
Capital-Labor Conflict

THROUGHOUT our country's history the workingman has sought to improve his condition. The principal workmen in the colonies were skilled craftsmen and their apprentices, and it was not until after the Revolutionary War and the break in the ties with England that industry expanded and a true working class came into being.

The development of manufacturing brought together large numbers of workers under one factory roof and in a single specialized industry. Trade unions were the result —the banding together for the improvement of their common welfare. A union's purpose was and still is to form means of contact and negotiation between employees and employers in a single work situation and, beginning in the latter half of the nineteenth century, in an entire industry.

The resulting struggle between capital and labor (or, more definitely, between employers and employees or management and workers) has been long and often violent. During the late 1800s industrial leaders almost uniformly resented the demands of workers and considered that their defiance represented nothing short of mutiny. The ideal situation from the standpoint of the management was a controlled and docile labor force who would accept unquestioningly any terms and conditions of work.

The strike, however, has always been the principal means of obtaining worker demands. With or without accompanying demonstrations or picketing, it may erupt into violence and, in extreme cases, into a full-scale riot. The sit-down or sit-down strike—a work stoppage in which employees refuse to leave their place of employment—is comparatively new in labor history. The employer equivalent of the sit-down is the lockout, in which management withholds employment by closing a plant or temporarily stopping its operation as a means of forcing workers to accept its terms.

A strike, in the definition of the United States Bureau of Labor Statistics, is "a temporary stoppage of work by a group of employees in order to express a grievance or to enforce a demand." A more emotionally tinged definition by a sympathetic pro-labor writer is "a practical protest, or a revolt, frequently successful, against wrongs which may be unendurable." These grievances and "wrongs" have traditionally involved unionization (open vs. closed shop), wages, hours of work, and working conditions. Strikes increase during eras of business prosperity, when wage demands stand a better than ordinary chance of acceptance. During a depression period strikers are apt to be in desperate economic straits and therefore tend to more mob violence.

Strike violence appears to follow a definite pattern. The strike begins with peaceful picketing after the leaders have appealed to their forces in favor of obedience to the law and the maintenance of order. Strikers are particularly warned against any resistance to legal authority, for this can inflame a crowd into mob action.

A strike of comparative calm is difficult to achieve when the hostility of each side to the other has been building up for a long time; the pre-strike negotiations often intensify this enmity. When obstinacy is met with obstinacy tempers become frayed and each side blames the other for the impasse. A self-appointed leader or agitator, or a persuasive orator, can arouse strikers, who are already showing their defiance, to unthinking and ill-advised actions.

Strike leaders are the first to admit that "a little violence"—a scuffle or altercation between strikers and police or strikers and non-union workers—is very often the means of winning a strike. Since all rioting springs from the feeling of bitter ill will, employers are usually pained and worried when strikers have reached this point; past history offers impressive examples of what might be expected to follow. The result is often a renewal of collective bargaining to the obvious advantage of the workers.

As in all riots, a particular incident or situation triggers the mob violence. In labor conflicts this is most often the hiring of non-union workmen (scabs) in place of the strikers. Resentment of the strikebreakers, often imported from outside the immediate strike area, stiffens the resistance and obstinacy of the strikers and may incite them to extreme and unrestrained acts. Sometimes an unyielding resistance on the part of the employers manifested by a threatening or challenging statement or an ill-timed act will lead to lawlessness.

In the 1892 strike of workers at the Carnegie Steel Company in Homestead, Pennsylvania, the violence, unparalleled in a labor-management dispute before or since, followed a long-planned lockout which was to have been enforced by a substantial number of hired and imported private police. The strikers reacted with savage violence against those brought into the community to protect strikebreakers. The Homestead lockout has been appropriately characterized as "one of the great battles for workers' rights" and "a battle which for bloodthirstiness and boldness could not be excelled in actual warfare."

Homestead, seven miles east of Pittsburgh on the south bank of the Monongahela River, was typical of many industrial towns just before the turn of the century. Of its population of 11,000, some 3,800 were employed in the plant of the Carnegie Steel Company, America's largest and most modern steel plant at the time.

The mill, fronting the curving waterfront for a mile, dominated the town. Operating around the clock, its chimneys continually belched out acrid and poisonous smoke, dust, dirt, and cinders (this was long before the subject of air pollution was even dreamed of), so that sunlight was seldom able to penetrate the ever present dark pall. At night the sky was lit by the blazing fires of the furnaces. The river water was contaminated by industrial wastes and sewage from upstream. Homestead was a desolate, dirty, and depressing town.

Conditions for the majority of the workers were deplor-

able. The unskilled day laborers (primarily Slavs, called
dinkey men or bohunks) were paid fourteen cents an
hour—$9.80 a week, the equivalent of less than $40 today.
However, the earnings of skilled laborers, the aristocrats
of the work force, were excellent—as much as $70 a week
($280 by today's standards). But all steelworkers more
than earned their wages. Working conditions were appalling: twelve-hour shifts, seven-day weeks, temperatures
of 130 degrees, no time out for meals, no washing-up
facilities, and no compensation for injuries. The year before the strike three hundred men were killed and two
thousand injured on the job in the mills around Pittsburgh
alone.

Only a fifth of the workers (about seven hundred) were
members of the industry union, the Amalgamated Association of Iron and Steel Workers, affiliated with the
American Federation of Labor. Andrew Carnegie, the
firm's head, was publicly on record as favoring unions
and approving them as a part of the ideal employer-
employee relationship. Privately he opposed them.

The company's chairman and general manager, Henry
Clay Frick, who was in charge of making and adminis-
tering policy, was an outspoken anti-unionist; he had
repeatedly stated that unions should not exist. In previous
clashes with organized labor when he was the "Coke
King" prior to joining forces with Carnegie, he had crushed
any worker opposition with force and made no concessions
whatsoever. He brought in deputy sheriffs, the state militia, and private Pinkerton detectives whenever he felt
they might be useful.

Six months after he joined Carnegie in 1889, Frick had

settled a strike at Homestead only by making concessions. His opposition to the Amalgamated union was therefore strengthened. The showdown came as soon as the three-year union-management contract approached its expiration date of June 30, 1892.

Frick "suggested" a reduction in tonnage rates (wages were based on production and the current price of steel). Since prices and profits were higher than at the time of the previous contract, the union bargainers asked for a comparatively small wage increase. Frick's reply was an ultimatum—his offer remained unchanged, and furthermore he insisted on an expiration date of January 1 rather than June 30. Since production was lower during the winter the wages would be smaller when the next contract came up for consideration. He set a June 24 deadline for acceptance. Carnegie was conveniently absent on vacation in Scotland during both the negotiations and the subsequent strike.

The union members called for a strike on July 2 and were joined by the three thousand non-union mechanics and common laborers. The battle lines were drawn. Frick had decided to break the union at Homestead. Even before the deadline date he had begun signing up skilled workers from other companies and, as his trump card, had recruited a force of three hundred armed Pinkerton detectives to protect the works and the imported scabs. These paid guards, from Chicago and New York, were to gather at Ashtabula, Ohio, on Lake Erie, a mid-point between the two cities, on the morning of July 5 and proceed by rail to Youngstown. From there they were to be transported at night by boat up the Monongahela River to

Homestead. Since it might prove illegal to bring an armed force into the state of Pennsylvania, the rifles, pistols, billy clubs, and ammunition were to be shipped separately. The guards were to be armed after they were within the state boundaries.

Frick agreed to pay five dollars per day for each man. In the meantime two barges were fitted up for the Pinkertons, one with bunks as a dormitory, the other with tables as a large dining room. Two steam tugs were engaged to tow the barges to the landing place on the Carnegie premises.

When the contract deadline was not met, Frick began to shut down the works. By the thirtieth of June the entire work force was locked out. To strengthen the security of the plant, a fence fifteen feet high was built around it, extending to the river's edge. This was of solid boards topped with barbed wire and with holes spaced along its three-mile length, presumably for armed guards.

Though Frick had asked for a force of county deputies to protect the plant, none could apparently be recruited, so the Pinkerton men were to be deputized once they had landed on the company property.

By July 5 the force of 316 Pinkertons had assembled at the designated spot below Homestead. In addition to the professionals, the motley crowd of "detectives" included toughs, criminals, jobless drifters, and college students on vacation. They were told only that they had been hired by a corporation as guards. They were armed with two hundred and fifty Winchester rifles, three hundred pistols, and ammunition. Like an army unit, they were dressed in uniforms of slouch hats with colorful bands and dark blue trousers with lighter stripes.

The strikers never for a moment underestimated the tactics Frick might employ, and so they established an elaborate system of scouts and guards to keep abreast of developments.

The expedition set out shortly after midnight on July 6, 1892, the two barges at first being towed by two tugs—then, after an engine failure, by one. Each Pinkerton man was armed and given fifty rounds of ammunition during the four-hour trip. But such a movement could scarcely remain secret, and a union lookout at Pittsburgh telegraphed Homestead: "Watch the river. Steamer with barges left here."

When the tug was approaching the spot selected for the landing inside the plant grounds, the pilot sounded the required steam whistle to indicate a landing. This was the signal for the town to come alive. Strikers joined citizens in rushing to the banks of the Monongahela River. Hundreds of armed strikers running along the shore fired into the pitch-blackness of the river. The approach to the river side of the plant, however, was blocked by the fence. In a single moment the crowd knocked over the obstruction and rushed pell-mell to the spot where the two barges were pulled up parallel to the shore line. At this time the protesters were estimated to number close to ten thousand men, women and boys, all bearing weapons—pistols, revolvers, rifles, clubs, sticks, or stones. At the landing all was strangely silent; each side appeared to be awaiting a first move by the other.

The leader of the Pinkerton forces shouted a warning that his men were coming ashore, he had hoped peacefully, to occupy the works. When the gangplank had been laid, several strikers attempted to dislodge it without success. Jeers and stones greeted the first rifle-carrying blue-clad enemy on the plank. But as more stepped forward (forty had volunteered) a hail of bullets killed one and seriously wounded five. Other Pinkertons returned the fire and their bullets found ready marks in the dense crowd. More than thirty fell wounded and two were killed instantly. The firing by both sides continued even after the guards sought shelter below deck. This first encounter had lasted only three minutes.

During the lull the strikers erected steel and wooden barriers at the top of the steep bank, the wounded and dead were removed, and the non-combatants and women moved away from the line of fire, to observe better the inevitable continuation of the battle. The Pinkerton tug meanwhile left for Pittsburgh with the wounded under a barrage of gunfire.

Daylight was approaching and the stalemate must be broken. A representative of the strikers attempted to obtain the surrender of the hirelings, but the answer, shouted to all within range, was "If you don't withdraw, we will mow every one of you down." At eight o'clock a second landing attempt resulted in more killed and wounded on both sides, and spasmodic firing continued for more than two more hours. But the Pinkerton men, sheltered below the decks of the barges, could only fire through the limited number of portholes, with little range.

Now the strikers and their sympathizers had gained

the advantage, and they sought to flush out their trapped quarry on the barges. Dynamite sticks proved effective only when thrown from nearby boats; even then the damage was slight. Civil War cannons were then fired from both sides of the river, but they, too, were relatively ineffective.

Then the strikers remembered the plant's oil stored in tanks. Pumping the oil into the river upstream from the barges, they attempted to start a fire without success. Next they ignited a raft loaded with greasy cloths and oil and cast it adrift, but the current floated the raft safely past the barges. Finally a small car loaded with blazing barrels of oil was rolled down the expanse of the bank but was deflected from its course before reaching the waterline. Sporadic gunfire continued during all these attempts at barge burning.

When the tug returned from Pittsburgh and tried to approach the barges to pull them free from the shore, the fire from the hundreds of armed strikers was so intense that it quickly retreated.

The impasse continued. The Pinkerton forces had several times waved white surrender handkerchiefs through portholes, only to have them shot away. For three afternoon hours the union and strike leaders attempted to reason with the mob, to convince them that further violence would inevitably lead to more casualties, and that nothing could possibly be gained by a continuation of the fighting. The more determined and excited strikers resisted these appeals. But the arguments of reason finally prevailed, and at about five o'clock the surrender negotiations were completed.

Before disembarking each guard was stripped of his pistol and jacket. When all three hundred were ashore, they huddled together in a frightened group while the strikers systematically pillaged the two barges of everything movable. The workers then set them afire and the crowd cheered lustily as they were burned to the waterline.

The Pinkerton prisoners had been promised safe passage through the plant to the Homestead railroad station and they started up the sloping bank to the accompaniment of only angry jeers, hoots, hisses, and howls. But the mob began a concentrated attack, surrounding groups and clubbing, beating, and kicking about forty of them into unconsciousness. There was no escape in running through this gauntlet of enraged men, women, and children who had seen some of their friends and relatives wounded or killed, and almost every one of the mercenaries was injured.

After being held under close guard in the town theater, the Pinkerton men finally entrained at midnight for Pittsburgh.

The casualties of this "shocking, sickening, uncivilized day" were never accurately totaled. The most reliable figure was at least thirty-five strikers and Pinkertons dead and four hundred injured, many of them seriously.

Frick's appeal to Governor Pattison for aid was not answered until July 12, when eight thousand Pennsylvania National Guardsmen marched in quietly to take over control of Homestead under martial law. The strikers were forced off the company's premises. With such protection Frick began bringing in scabs and proceeded to file charges against the strike leaders for the attack on the Pinkertons. Public sympathy was overwhelmingly in favor of the strikers, and the juries in the first three murder trials voted for acquittal. No more were brought to trial. An additional 167 strikers were indicted, but the charges were eventually dropped.

The troops remained until mid-October, at which time two thousand non-union strikebreakers were well on the road to re-establishing full production. By November the Amalgamated treasury was empty and the strike was abandoned. The union members did not get their jobs back. The union was broken; and not until 1935, with the formation of the Congress of Industrial Organizations (CIO) did the nation's steelworkers effectively organize again.

Henry C. Frick, sworn enemy of unionism, had carried out his threat. Furthermore, only some eight hundred of the original non-union working force were reinstated, for Frick was not one to forgive and forget. An anarchist from New York, Alexander Berkman, inflamed by newspaper accounts of the strike, forced his way into Frick's office in Pittsburgh and attempted to assassinate him. Although shot and stabbed, the autocratic magnate survived. After the strike he and Carnegie became bitter enemies.

The Homestead strike was not a spontaneous uprising on the part of unorganized workers. It was a war between one of the most powerful of the great modern corporations (the expanding Carnegie Steel Company became the United States Steel Corporation) and what was then one of the strongest unions in the country.

The company won and the riotous strikers lost in what

was one of the more tragic chapters in the history of United States labor-management relations.

Homestead and Pullman (Chapter 9) are but two of the major strikes in American labor history which have included full-scale riots. Among others were the national railroad strike of 1877; the Chicago McCormick Reaper strike (1886) which triggered the Haymarket riot, with the first bombing in American labor history; that of the Pennsylvania anthracite coal miners in 1902; the national steel strike of 1919; the coal miners' national strike in 1922; and the west coast longshoremen's walkout in 1934.

All have shown the determination of the unions to achieve the best possible conditions of and rewards for work. The rioters in industrial strikes have possessed an unequaled desperation, and the gains of the laboring man, painfully achieved step by step, form a record of frustrations and failures as well as successes.

The Great Railroad Boycott

THE FIRST great nationwide railroad strike in 1877 began as a protest against a wage cut in Baltimore and involved many separate riots affecting various railroads, and it spread to the Pacific coast. Before the strike ended, millions of dollars in property had been destroyed and more than one hundred were dead.

The next large strike of railway workers began, similarly, as a local union-management struggle in the town of Pullman, Illinois, spreading until it covered two thirds of the United States.

The strike was astonishing, for at the time the Pullman Palace Car Company enjoyed an excellent public image because of its model company town, Pullman, twelve miles south of the Chicago business district. The company, founded in 1867 by George Pullman, manufactured and operated under contract both parlor and sleeping cars. In 1880 construction of the ideal community was begun: "to build, in close proximity to the shops, homes for workingmen of such character and surrround-

ings as would prove so attractive as to cause the best class
of mechanics to seek that place for employment in preference to others . . ." and "would result in a tendency
toward continued elevation and improvement of the conditions not only of the working people themselves, but of
their children growing up."

A profit motive, however, was behind this Utopian
town, which was completed in 1884. All prices charged
workers, for rent, for gas and water, for merchandise in
stores, and the like, were fixed so as to earn six per cent
on the investment. Furthermore, the rents for company
homes were twenty to twenty-five per cent higher than in
Chicago and other neighboring communities. While not
actually required to live in Pullman, workers were subtly
made to understand that those who did were more sure
of steady employment with the company.

The Pullman Company had never recognized a labor
organization. Before 1893 unions of railroad workers were
organized by types of work—locomotive engineers, firemen, trainmen, conductors, and switchmen—called brotherhoods. The need for a more inclusive single organization
resulted in the founding of the American Railway Union
in mid-1893. Eugene V. Debs, formerly of the Brother-
hood of Locomotive Firemen, became its president. Its
growth was rapid; within a year the membership was
greater than the combined brotherhoods.

More than half of the six thousand Pullman employees
joined the ARU in its first year. The depression of 1893
made it necessary for the company to lay off half the
workers and to cut by twenty per cent the wages of those
kept on, without any corresponding reduction in rents

and other services. The consequences were disastrous. After the company had made its deductions the average pay per worker was six dollars a week (equal in purchasing power to twenty-four dollars today)! Yet the company continued to pay dividends which were actually increased. Particularly galling to the workers was the fact that salaries of the officers and managers, the top-level employees, were untouched.

The festering discontent of the workers finally expressed itself in May 1894, when an employee committee requested that, since business had improved, the old wage level should be restored. The refusal was curt, and to show the management's displeasure with "chronic trouble-makers," three of the committee were discharged on May 10. The Pullman workers in Chicago walked out on strike the next day and appealed to the ARU for support. The non-union workers were promptly laid off, and the plant was shut down.

American Railway Union President Debs attempted without success to persuade the Pullman Company to arbitrate. On June 26 the union began a sympathetic boycott, its sixty thousand members on the Western railway lines refusing to handle Pullman cars. Pullman and all traffic from Chicago ceased. The boycott then spread slowly to the South and East so that the field of operations of the strike, originally only the Chicago area, extended from the Allegheny Mountains to the Pacific Ocean. Chicago, however, became the central battleground, and the riots within the city were continuous and violent.

Then as now, Chicago was the most important and busiest railroad center in the country. Twenty-four lines terminated or centered in the city; approximately three thousand miles of railway track were within its limits. The area was filled with yards, shops, roundhouses, signal towers, and switching systems—all perfect targets for rioters bent on destruction.

While the actual strike at Pullman began on May 11, there was no hint of trouble of any kind in Chicago until June 27, the day after the American Railway Union's boycott became effective. To prevent any passenger or freight trains from leaving or entering Chicago, strikers uncoupled engines from trains and switchmen obstructed the main tracks with single cars or threw switches so that trains would be shunted to dead-end sidings. The scab engineers and firemen were pulled from their cabs, conductors were threatened with bodily violence. A few trains were derailed, further blocking traffic.

These activities were mainly the work of the strikers, who were later to be joined by sympathizers in more destructive activities. For the next four days the only "riotous" acts within the city limits were stone throwing, hooting, and hissing at the non-union replacement scabs. In response to appeals from the General Railway Managers' Association, an organization of the Chicago lines, the city police were successful in preventing the assembly of any sizable group which might be bent on mob violence. However, outbreaks at Blue Island, an outlying village to the south, were very serious, and an uncontrolled mob was successful in halting the operations of the Rock Island Railroad.

To protect railroad property the Managers' Association requested the United States marshal in Chicago to appoint deputy marshals. By the first of July between fifteen hundred and two thousand had been recruited. They were to be paid by the railroads and were company employees as well as United States peace officers.

Even such large numbers, however, could not prevent the strikers' interference with train movements, and by June 28 all twenty-four railroads were paralyzed. The introduction of these special deputies laid down the battle lines and was the signal for the beginning of violence. Freight cars were derailed, overturned, or burned in increasing numbers.

All freight as well as passenger traffic was halted. Supplies of meat from the Chicago stockyards and the great packing houses were ruined by the heat or stolen from the halted trains. No provisions were able to reach the city. An actual embargo upon the commerce of Chicago existed. From a legal standpoint this constituted interference with interstate commerce. The United States mail was also tied up; mail cars were idle. Attorney General Richard Olney accordingly began to lay the groundwork for government action against the strikers and boycotters.

Olney felt that vigorous federal interference in Chicago, the origin and center of the strike, would prevent its spread over the entire country. One of the many accusations made by the union following the strike was that the government's first act in Chicago was a definite alliance with the railway interests, for Olney was a railroad lawyer and member of the board of several lines. The authorization to employ deputies was only the first step, Olney said, "but the true way of dealing with the matter is by a force which is overwhelming and prevents any attempt at resistance."

The result was a "first" in the history of American

labor—the issuance of a federal injunction to stop a labor dispute. The Attorney General explained the basis of the order: "A railway is not a mere private enterprise; it is a public highway. Any obstruction in that highway can be dealt with by federal authorities as a restraint of commerce. Employees who in concert quit work on highways are in reality obstructing it; they can be dealt with as a conspiracy in restraint of trade." The "interference with the mails" was a violation of the Sherman Anti-Trust Act.

Two federal judges in Chicago accordingly issued an injunction on Monday, July 2, ordering all persons "to refrain from interfering or stopping any of the business of any of the railroads in Chicago engaged as common carriers."

When federal agents went to Blue Island to read the injunction to a crowd of from two to three thousand who had that morning blocked the Rock Island tracks, they were jeered at. The exhilarated crowd yelled, "To hell with the government! To hell with the Court!" When some of the mob threw themselves in front of an engine to stop its progress, the deputy marshals opened fire. The ensuing affray resulted in the stabbing of one marshal and the wounding of several others. When this defiant outburst was reported to President Grover Cleveland, he accepted his Attorney General's suggestion and ordered federal troops to Chicago. Neither the governor of Illinois nor the mayor of Chicago was consulted on this move.

The first troops, numbering five hundred, arrived in Chicago on July 4.

Because of the increasing tenseness of the strike, people

began to gather on railroad property out of curiosity to see what might happen. The later federal investigation noted that there was seldom any purpose or leadership in the mobs; most of the destruction, the report stated, was "done wantonly and without premeditation." As in most riots, many hoodlums and young boys were among the most active. In Chicago a large number of women participated also.

Because of the dense mass of men, women, and children blocking the way, half a battalion of the first soldiers from nearby Fort Sheridan found it necessary to advance to their duty posts at the Union Stockyards on the evening of their arrival with rifles leveled and revolvers ready. In spite of their vigilance while guarding railway personnel in clearing the tracks to restore service, trains were uncoupled, many by women; cars were derailed; Pullmans were sidetracked; and several freight cars were burned that evening.

Because of the many separate tracks and yards scattered on the south side of the city, the limited number of troops could not control the many separate mobs who might easily overturn and burn cars in one spot and disperse before police or soldiers could arrive. For that reason Mayor John Hopkins on Thursday, July 5, asked Governor John Altgeld to send immediately to Chicago such state militia (National Guard) troops as were available "to aid in suppressing and preventing continued violence to persons and property." The governor immediately ordered two thousand of the militiamen to the city. Within two or three days more than four thousand were on active duty there.

On the fifth of July large crowds roamed almost at will, pushing over freight cars, setting a few of them on fire, throwing switches, stoning trains, and burning signal towers. At one spot the soldiers dispersed a huge crowd at bayonet point. In the evening at the stockyards the crowd was estimated to number ten thousand. No firearms were used because such orders had not yet been issued. The commanders were sensibly awaiting developments.

During the evening of the fifth a colossal fire engulfed the buildings of the 1892 World's Columbian Exposition at Jackson Park. The overworked fire department was being summoned here and there where freight cars were blazing, and seven buildings were reduced to ashes before the conflagration was brought under control. Though the blaze was undoubtedly the work of an incendiary, the citizens, encouraged by the newspapers, quite naturally assumed that the strikers, or at least their sympathizers, were the guilty ones.

The peak of destruction was reached on Friday, July 6, when mobs destroyed railroad property valued at $340,000 (more than $1,250,000 at today's values). By this time hundreds of freight cars which had been stopped on various tracks were grouped together in the individual companies' yards, where they could be more easily guarded by both the federal soldiers and the state militiamen. These yards were in the southern section of the city, generally removed from any concentrations of buildings or houses. But the very extent of the long rows lining the tracks of the various sidings made car-to-car guarding impossible and led to a "carnival of incendiarism." The axle boxes of freight cars were filled with greasy rags and waste; anyone could secrete himself between or in the cars when a guard passed, then remove this waste, apply a match, and possess an ideal torch.

Because the day was breezy, it was not even necessary to set each car afire; the wind would fan the flames through the tightly packed cars. Since the fire hoses could seldom reach the lines of flames, complete destruction was achieved with a minimum of activity. The mob became observers encouraging and cheering the relatively few actual fire setters. Those at the Illinois Central yards within the city limits were particularly vengeful because one of the company's agents had shot and seriously wounded two trespassing rioters at the stockyards the night before.

The greatest destruction of freight cars in a single yard took place on this Friday evening, when fires destroyed more than seven hundred cars at the Panhandle yards at Fiftieth Street in South Chicago. The yard was one of the largest—two miles long and a half mile wide—and the tracks were packed solidly with freight cars. The surrounding rural area was completely open, with no fences, barriers, or buildings. For some reason never explained, only a token force of soldiers and militiamen had been assigned there. Because of its isolation, no hydrants were installed along the tracks. The rioters found in it an unparalleled opportunity for unimpeded destruction. The mob there was said to have numbered six thousand.

The Chicago *Inter Ocean* reported the successful activities of the mob: "From this moving mass of shouting rioters squads of a dozen or two departed, running toward the yards with fire brands in their hands. They looked in the gloaming like specters, their lighted torches bobbing about like will-o'-the-wisps. Soon from all parts of the yard flames shot up and billows of fire rolled over the cars, covering them with the red glow of destruction. The spectacle was a grand one. . . . Before the cars were fired those filled with any cargoes were looted. . . . The people were bold, shameless, and eager in their robbery. . . . It was pandemonium let loose, the fire leaping along for miles and the men and women dancing with frenzy. It was a mad scene where riot became wanton and men and women became drunk on their excesses."

The light of dawn showed long, continuous rows of blackened wheels and undercarriages, and tracks twisted and broken by the intense heat.

Up to this time most of the casualties had been inflicted by the federal marshals and troops. During this Friday the state militiamen began pouring into the city in response to Governor Altgeld's call. They were scattered in small companies for the purpose of clearing the tracks, protecting railroad property, and restoring order.

This action precipitated the most violent encounter of the entire Chicago strike period. While furnishing protection to a wrecking train on the Grand Trunk line at Forty-ninth and Loomis streets on the afternoon of July 7, a company of the Illinois National Guard was attacked by an angry mob. A contemporary account, again in *Inter Ocean*, describes the encounter:

"Several thousand people had been following the train and, as their number increased, many became bolder. Approaching Loomis Street, the train halted to raise a car which had been overturned. The crowd hooted and swore at the soldiers, throwing stones and bricks. A few shots were fired. After warning the crowd to disperse, the commander ordered his troops to load their rifles. For the moment this seemed to have a salutary effect, causing a few women and children to leave, but in reality generating an uglier spirit among the rioters. The hail of stones continued without interruption.

"A bayonet charge was immediately ordered, during which some rioters were severely wounded. However, this cleared the railroad right of way. More determined than ever to resist the progress of the train, the mob returned, some of whom rushed forward and upset a flat car which had just been righted. More missiles were hurled and some shots fired by the rioters. Four soldiers had already been severely wounded and the lieutenant injured in the head by a stone. No reinforcements had appeared. The situation was perilous; there seemed to be no alternative left to the commanding officer except to order his men to fire at will and to make every shot count."

The several volleys of the soldiers killed four and wounded twenty rioters. Some of the latter were women. The stunned crowd was dispersed by the city police in a series of charges with drawn revolvers, but without the firing of another shot.

The Loomis Street confrontation marked the peak of the Chicago violence. It was also another tragic landmark in the history of American labor—the first time United States troops fired on workers.

Because of the continued outbreaks of violence, President Cleveland was pressed to declare martial law. This he hesitated to do. Instead, on July 8 he issued a proclamation to the people of Illinois and of Chicago in particular, warning them that those "taking part with a riotous mob in forcibly resisting and obstructing the execution of the laws . . . cannot be regarded otherwise than as public enemies."

By now the forces of law and order in the city had reached a total of more than fourteen thousand, including city police (three thousand), Illinois state militiamen (four thousand), United States soldiers (two thousand), and five thousand federal marshals and their deputies. The presidential proclamation and the show of strength calmed the strikers and their followers. Within a week most of the railway workers had returned to their jobs. The Pullman shops reopened on August 2, the day the unsuccessful strike was called off by a conference of union delegates.

The generally accepted casualty total was 13 killed and 53 seriously injured. Arrests by federal officers totaled 190, but only 71 were upheld, and few rioters were brought to trial. Eugene Debs and other leaders of the American Railway Union were arrested and tried for contempt and conspiracy. Debs served six months in prison; this marked the beginning of his national prominence in American labor.

Only the Chicago phase of the nationwide strike has been discussed here. But violence was everywhere—in Illinois, in Indiana, Iowa, Oklahoma, Colorado, Utah, New Mexico, and California. The boycott did not affect the Northeast because Pullman did not hold contracts with those railroads. Sixteen thousand soldiers were stationed throughout the country at the height of the strike and terror tactics were frequent, though not on such a vast and destructive scale as in Chicago.

The Pullman strike and its resulting national boycott have been called an almost unparalleled labor upheaval, with all union members standing solidly together to cripple the operations of their employers. Seldom have multiple mobs been so destructive in fighting the enemy—in this case the railroad managers—only to lose the battle in the end.

The losses to the railroads totaled over five million dollars, including property damage and loss of earnings. The strikers forfeited almost a million and a half dollars in wages.

Eugene Debs and his American Railway Union fared badly at the time. Railroad detectives prevented his organizing activities and, recognizing defeat, the ARU was organized in 1897 for political action as the Social Democratic Party, the forerunner of the Socialist Party of America.

The investigation of the causes of the strike by the United States Strike Commission made recommendations for improving labor relations in the railroad industry, but the managers failed to agree on many of them.

Worst of all to George Pullman was the liquidation of his beloved model town into an ordinary factory town.

> ## MINERS' RIOT
> ### Coeur d'Alene District, Idaho
> #### April 29, 1899

Explosion at Bunker Hill

FROM ITS earliest days the mining industry of our country has suffered continuously from labor unrest. The major problems have been two—unionization and wages—and no segment of the industry has been exempt. Coal, iron, copper, lead, zinc, gold, and silver workers have all at one time or another resorted to violence to gain their demands. The frequency of miners' strikes may be partially explained by the unusual and hazardous conditions of work.

The underground workers, in contrast to surface miners, run great risks to both their safety and their health. Only when unionized have miners been able to improve their wages and working conditions. As in most other industries, the struggle for union recognition has been filled with desperation, bitterness, hatred, and violence on the part of both owners and workers.

The dispute through the two last decades of the nineteenth century was brought on in part by the unyielding opposition of some mine owners and operators to unionization of their plants and their refusal to discuss the matter with worker representatives. Union agents were considered mortal enemies of management and dismissed contemptuously as irresponsible troublemakers. Nuisances they were, for their type of local union organization often involved rousing the workers into a frenzy of discontent.

The major national miners' union was the United Mine Workers of America, formed in 1849; but its activity, particularly in coal, was limited to the eastern and central states. Unionization of miners in the western states was vigorously pressed by the Western Federation of Miners, which had close Socialist Party affiliations and after the turn of the century was to be connected with the leftist International Workers of the World (the IWW or Wobblies). This union's activities in northwestern Idaho during the 1890s were so violent and disturbing that within eight years three successive presidents were called upon by as many worried governors to dispatch United States troops to preserve the peace—Harrison in 1892, Cleveland in 1894, and McKinley in 1899.

The mines of the Coeur d'Alene district were in Shoshone County, Idaho, near the northern end of the Panhandle of the state. This was one of the richest lead-mining regions in the world, the ore carrying considerable silver. Lead was first discovered in the county in 1882. Six shanty towns were strung along the base of barren mountains; in some there was room for only a single narrow street between the mountains and the deep canyon creek. The only routes in and out were the Northern Pacific and Oregon Railway & Navigation Company railroads. The small mining towns along these railroads from east to west were Mullan, Gem, Burke, Wallace, and Kellogg; a three-mile spur line led to Wardner.

By 1892 quarrels between the operators and their employees were frequent. Efforts of the union to force an increase in the wage level caused the operators to import non-union workers, scabs. The riot in July at Homestead, Pennsylvania (Chapter 8), was reported to have encouraged the Coeur d'Alene miners to resort to violence. On July 11 armed union men attacked the guards and workmen at the Frisco mine in Gem, three of the latter being killed. The mill of the mine was blown up. The governor proclaimed martial law and requested federal troops, who remained in the area until mid-November. More than three hundred men were arrested, but none was punished. Small wage increases resulted.

Spurred by the Pullman strike, two years later (Chapter 9), the union members undertook a campaign of intimidation and terrorism. Forty masked men shot and killed one of the principal 1892 state witnesses in the Frisco mine case, kidnaped a mine superintendent, and attempted to blow up a mine at Wardner. Federal troops were again summoned and remained for three weeks.

The policy of harassment on non-union miners continued without interference by the local law officers, and by 1899 the only mine in the district not unionized was that of the Bunker Hill and Sullivan Company at Wardner. In April the employees were met and threatened by armed men and required to join the union. The company then raised the pay to meet the union scale in effect at the other mines but refused to recognize the union.

This rejection could not be tolerated by the Coeur

d'Alene Miners' Union, which for many years had fought
to prevent the employment of any person other than its
members in these regional mines. Bunker Hill and Sullivan
was the last holdout. Its operators must be reminded, by
force if necessary, that this situation would no longer be
tolerated.

On the morning of Saturday, April 29, which was not a
working day, the members of all locals—Mullan, Gem,
Burke, and Wardner—met to discuss a course of action.
Since the same blueprint plan was outlined to each group,
they simultaneously decided to go to Wardner, armed and
masked or unmasked according to individual choice.

The Mullan members, two hundred strong, marched
seven miles west to Wallace, collecting guns and ammunition previously stored at farms along the road. Meanwhile two hundred of the Burke local seized a Northern
Pacific train of nine freight and ore cars and forced the
engineer to proceed at reduced speed. Seven miles farther
on, at Gem, a hundred and fifty to two hundred men
awaited the train. As it stopped a dozen excited men
jumped off and walked a few yards to the storehouse of
the Helena-Frisco Mining Company, threatened the manager, and seized eighty kegs of dynamite (about three
thousand pounds).

It was ten-thirty when the train reached Wallace, three
miles beyond, where the waiting Mullan members climbed
aboard. The train proceeded another twelve miles to
Kellogg, where it was switched to the O. R. & N. Company
tracks for the last lap of the journey, the three miles to
Wardner. About a mile from town the Wardner members
who had left the town in groups of three to ten joined

their comrades. By that time, about 1 P.M., the crowd numbered about a thousand (two thirds of the total membership), about half of whom were masked and armed with Winchester rifles and pistols. The cars were packed and men even clung to the engine and tender.

When the "Dynamite Express," as the train was later called, stopped at the Wardner station the previously prepared plan was carried out with military precision; the group at this time was far from being a disorganized mob. The men were lined up, the orders shouted "Burke Union to the front," "Gem Union to the front," and the same for the others. Each miner wore either a strip of white handkerchief in the buttonhole of his coat or a strip of white cloth tied on his right arm. For nearly an hour the "at ease" men occupied the time by passing around bottles of whiskey, while the leaders conferred on the next moves and strategy.

This waiting period was the beginning of the transformation of the crowd into a mob, for the individuals, united in a single well-defined purpose, began to become emboldened and reckless. One and all, they believed that they could destroy the Bunker Hill Mine and kill its superintendent, who had acted as spokesman for the operators, with no fear of punishment, that, in short, they "could get away with it." This belief was enforced by the fact that the county sheriff, whose pro-union sympathies were well known, was present and was apparently to offer no opposition.

After almost an hour the boxcar containing the dynamite was opened, and the kegs containing a ton and a half of powder were distributed to the various detachments. An advance armed guard of about a hundred and fifty (hoping to flush out the hated superintendent) riddled the office building with bullets, but he had been forewarned and had escaped. Meanwhile a small band crept along the creek and fired a few shots at the mine's concentrator, a complicated plant where the wastes were removed from rough ore. Mistaking them for Bunker Hill men, the main body riddled them with bullets, killing a member of the Burke local, named Smythe.

While one group was spreading the dynamite through the mill and office and under the concentrator, another was setting fire to the company's boardinghouse and bunkhouse as well as the superintendent's home. The majority of the visitors had marched together from the railroad station to the mine, and they encouraged the active groups with cheers. Soon the cry of "Fire!" drove them back to the single main street. Everyone shouted, "Farther back! They're going to put on the show! Out of the way!" The long-awaited moment had arrived. The fuses were ready and the destruction of one of the largest concentrators in the world was about to begin.

At 2:26 P.M. the fuses were lighted and the concentrator was blown skyward in pieces, accompanied by a cloud of dust and smoke and followed by a deafening roar that could be heard twenty miles away. Broken fragments of machinery and timbers from the building were hurled high into the air. Fifteen seconds later another blast shattered the office building. From the force of the third, debris was hurled in every direction.

The work of destruction was complete; the great Bunker Hill mill, valued at $250,000, was totally destroyed.

As if awed by what they had seen, the watching union members were silent for a few moments. Then almost instantaneously the crowd was transformed into a mob. One and all they yelled like demons as they gloried in their accomplishment. A celebration was in order, and suddenly those with rifles and revolvers began shooting into the air as they started the short walk back to the train.

Unfortunately two of the non-union men of the Bunker Hill mine were identified by the Wardner organizer, and the mob moved upon them for the fun of punishment. For over an hour they held prisoner James Cheyne, a millman, and Roger Rogers, the company's stenographer, forcing them to run on command, kicking them, striking them with their guns, and threatening their lives. Finally, as the train whistle signaled the approaching time of departure, they crowned these indignities by ordering their two terrified captives to run, then firing as near to them as possible. As the two stumbled on the run a hail of bullets surrounded them, some dangerously near to their heels. The aim of some tipsy celebrants was naturally inaccurate, and Rogers' lip was torn by a bullet, while Cheyne was shot in the hip. He lay bleeding in the road, for anyone attempting to aid him was himself threatened. Finally a woman defied the attackers and made him comfortable until the attackers went to the station.

The fun was over. The jubilation was somewhat dampened when the body of their fellow member Smythe was brought down from the mountainside and placed in the baggage car. But of course it was understood by everyone that the shooting was accidental, though regrettable, and the train began the return trip.

But about half a mile from Wardner someone discovered that some seventy-five men had been left behind, so the train backed up for them. The passengers were dropped off at their home stations. By five o'clock the train was at Burke, its starting point, and the local men removed Smythe's body. The day had been an unqualified success; the destruction had proceeded according to schedule and the Bunker Hill operators had been given to understand that if they rebuilt and recommenced operations they would be wise to recognize the union.

Repercussions were immediate. By evening Idaho Governor Frank Steunenberg appealed to President McKinley for federal troops, since most of the state's National Guard forces were in the Philippines. Within three days five hundred soldiers were in the area. On May 3 the Governor declared martial law in Shoshone County.

Now began the task of arresting those involved in the incident. Many were able to escape to Montana, but the soldiers and local deputies, visiting each mining camp, were able to round up more than seven hundred who were held in military custody for pre-trial hearings. The first few hundred were jailed in a large hay warehouse; those arrested later were held in boxcars. The number finally held for trial was about five hundred. The coroner's jury laboriously examined hundreds of witnesses, focusing on the two murders (Cheyne died on May 2) "under riotous conditions" rather than the blowing up of the mine. Honest testimony was difficult to obtain because of wide-

spread fear, and therefore only the principal offenders
were eventually brought to trial. Most of the union leaders
fled from the state; the one organizer arrested was tried
for conspiracy and murder and sentenced to imprisonment for seventeen years. Thirteen miners were also tried
and ten found guilty, serving short terms. The federal
troops remained in the area until the end of October.

The uprising of April 29, 1899 gained nothing for the
local of the Western Federation of Miners. Under state
supervision the operators of the mines of the Coeur d'Alene
district banded together to screen all union workers so
that those involved in any way were required to obtain
work permits when the mines reopened ten days after
the explosion. Each man appeared before state agents
and signed application forms which called for an answer
to the specific question: "I did not participate actively
or otherwise in the April 29th riots. Believing that the
crimes committed at Wardner were actively incited, encouraged and perpetrated through and by means of the
influence and direction of the Miners' Union, I hereby
express my unqualified disapproval of said acts, and
hereby renounce and forever abjure all allegiance to
said Miners' Union, of which I was a former member,
and I solemnly pledge myself to obey the law and not
again seek membership in any society which will encourage or tolerate any violation of law." Non-union
members signed application forms stating that they had
not participated in the Wardner violence.

The reign of intimidation and terror was temporarily
ended. However, so implacable and bitter was the feeling
of the Western Federation against Governor Steunenberg,

who continued his crackdown on miners' strikes during the remaining year of his administration, that in December 1905 he was killed by a bomb thrown by a professional assassin hired by the Federation.

The Shoshone County sheriff, who had openly aided the union members and "looked the other way," was removed from office, as were the county commissioners. A full-scale investigation by the Military Affairs Committee of the United States House of Representatives in 1900 endorsed the actions of President McKinley and Governor Steunenberg and approved the conduct of the troops during their long period of duty in the Coeur d'Alene district.

Coeur d'Alene was only one of the riot-torn strikes of miners in the long fight for union recognition. Two of the most bitter involved coal miners in Illinois and Kentucky. At Herrin, Illinois, in 1922, riotous violence during a strike cost thirty-six lives, twenty-one of them non-union miners. For two decades before unionization in 1941, the coal miners in Harlan County, Kentucky, engaged in bitter strife with the operators. So frequent were the outbreaks that the county gained the nickname "Bloody Harlan." Riots by coal miners were reduced when the majority of operators recognized the United Mine Workers of America, formed in 1890; John L. Lewis was its President for forty years, from 1920 to 1960.

RACE RIOT
East St. Louis, Ill.
July 2, 1917

Target of Prejudice: The Negro

As THE largest racial minority in the United States, the Negroes have been most persecuted by their white fellow citizens. Many times since the Civil War the most hideous and shocking of all outbreaks of mob violence—lynching and the race riot—have made Negroes their victims.

Lynchings of individual Negroes since 1900 have totaled about eighteen hundred but have become less and less frequent in recent years. None were reported in 1960 and 1962, and only one in 1961. The term "lynching" derived from the acts of Judge Charles Lynch, a Virginia justice of the peace who, during the American Revolution in 1780, caused British loyalists to be flogged without giving them recourse to due process of law.

In present usage, lynching is defined as "punishment meted out to individuals by unauthorized groups acting outside the law." The "punishment" has almost always been hanging. Lynching was the punishment most often meted out to lawbreakers in United States frontier communities before regularly constituted law forces were in control. The most famous use of lynching in the West was by the vigilantes of San Francisco in the 1850s. The victims of these frontier lynchings were mostly white.

The Negro lynching party is a small-scale riot in which the victim is the prey of a group too small in number to be called a mob, since the word implies a crowd, yet in action has all the characteristics of a mob. Lynchings have very often been part of larger race riots.

Deep-seated animosities against non-whites have caused other minority groups of foreign birth or heritage to suffer from mob action. An example of the anti-Chinese feeling on the Pacific coast is narrated in Chapter 7.

A legacy of the days of Spanish California was enmity toward Mexicans. Their lot as migrant laborers has been unhappy. In at least one serious riot, in wartime Los Angeles in 1943, they, together with Negroes, were the targets of violence by servicemen because of their unique "ducktail" haircuts and exaggerated clothing—fingertip-length coats, peg-leg trousers, and wide-brimmed hats. The avowed purpose was to show the "zoot-suiters" their place.

The antagonists in a race riot are usually aroused by a rumor or an incident that serves to release long-repressed hatreds and resentments; release is found in the comparative anonymity of a mob.

The attackers in the 1917 outbreak in East St. Louis, Illinois, committed acts of barbarity and savagery unmatched in other race riots, for East St. Louis represents the early twentieth century's peak of anti-Negro violence and brutality.

In 1917 East St. Louis, across the Mississippi River

from St. Louis, Missouri, was a railroad and industrial
center. Twenty-seven rail lines passed through or terminated in the city, and the major industries included the
large stockyards and meat packing plants of three major
companies and the huge works of the Aluminum Ore
Company and the American Steel Company. East St.
Louis profited from the wartime economy, and the con-
tinual need for more and more workers was responsible
for the growth in the Negro population from 6,000 (of a
59,000 total) in 1910 to 13,000 (of 70,000) in 1917. More
than two thousand Southern Negroes arrived in the year
before the riot.

This influx was the result of labor needs and the anti-
unionism of the major industries. Negro workers had been
recruited and imported in large numbers to replace strikers
at the packing (mid-1916) and aluminum (April 1917)
plants. Rumors that thousands more were to be imported
caused resentment and a call for action barring further
Negro migration.

In an open meeting before the City Council on the
evening of May 28, labor leaders harangued an overflow
crowd with inflammatory speeches, planting the seeds of
fear that their job security would be further threatened.
The crowd was restless and, according to the pattern of
riots, needed only a rumor or incident to release its hatred
and resentment.

A rumor was not long in coming. As the group left City
Hall, someone reported that a Negro had shot a white
man in a holdup. As the story spread, new rumors and
elaborations were added, all involving white girls and

women (a favorite device guaranteed to excite even the most latent anti-Negro feelings).

Within a short time more than three thousand persons had rushed downtown, with the common intention of beating every Negro unfortunate enough to be in the area. After beating and kicking scores of victims, the persecutors destroyed a few of the saloons and businesses catering to Negroes. Though two or three Negroes were shot and many beaten, no one was killed.

The attacks might have continued the next day had not several companies of the Illinois National Guard arrived in response to the pleas of the panic-stricken mayor. Even so, a good many colored citizens were assaulted. The understaffed local police force proved to be anti-Negro, the mayor hesitant about taking decisive action against the white voters who had elected him. This minor race riot was unfortunately not followed by any actions which might have relieved the tense situation. The caldron of prejudice was simmering and inevitably would boil over.

The incident that led to the July riot followed the usual pattern of a clash between Negroes and police. Since the May outbreak the beatings of Negroes had continued unchecked. Rumor stated that the East St. Louis Negroes were biding their time until July 4 when they would rise up against the whites. Conversely, this same rumor was circulated by the Negroes; the whites, it maintained, were planning an all-out attack.

In this atmosphere of mutual suspicion a Negro shot his white attacker on the night of July 1. A number of vengeful whites in a Ford automobile fired shots into

Negro homes, and on a second trip the fire was returned. When a police car, also a Ford, was sent to the spot to investigate, the Negroes again opened fire, killing one detective instantly and wounding a second so seriously that he died the next day. The murders were undoubtedly the result of mistaken identity, the two Fords and their occupants appearing the same in the darkness, but this mattered little at the time. This time the mayor was wise enough to call for the aid of state militia forces.

The next morning, Monday, July 2, 1917, the bullet-marked Ford, its bloodstained interior a vivid proof of the night's tragedy, was placed on exhibit in front of the main police station. Speakers at a hurriedly called early morning meeting urged "all worthy citizens" to arm themselves for afternoon action. Then they marched to the central part of the city and set the riot in motion by shooting the first Negro.

In view of hundreds of white spectators who were themselves either too frightened to interfere or frankly sympathetic to the actions of the white attackers, the rioters, at that time only small separate bands, followed a half-mile path of terror en route to the segregated Negro district, stoning and clubbing any man, woman, or child of color. The lack of interference and the apparent support of the citizen bystanders encouraged increasingly vicious acts. In the early afternoon several Negroes who had already been beaten and lay on the street unconscious were shot and killed. Dozens of Negro women were kicked by white women who beat them continuously with fists, stones, and sticks.

The midafternoon focus of the rioters was the scene of the May riot. The shacks of the poorer Negroes who lived there were surrounded and set afire. The incendiaries discovered the monstrous fun of shooting the residents as they appeared through the smoke and flames. This game was described by a St. Louis reporter:

"A crazed Negro would dash from his burning home, sometimes with a revolver in his hand. Immediately revolvers by the score would be fired. He would zig-zag through the spaces between buildings. Then a well-directed shot would strike him. He would leap into the air. There were deep shouts, intermingled with shrill feminine ones. The flames would creep to the body. The Negro would writhe, attempt to get up, more shots would be fired. The flames would eat their way to and past him."

The climax of the riot was reached during the early evening. By that time scores of Negro homes lay in ashes, yet the mob continued this game of burning and "nigger hunting" with undiminished glee. The hoses of the fire department were cut by axes and rendered useless. At least half a dozen children or seriously wounded men were hurled into the flames, to be burned to a crisp. "In one case," a witness testified, "a little ten-year-old boy, whose mother had been shot down, was running around sobbing and looking for her. Some members of the mob shot the boy, and before life had passed from his body they picked the little fellow up and threw him in the flames." In another incident, "a colored woman with a little two-year-old baby in her arms was trying to protect the child, and they shot her and also shot the child,

and threw them into the fire." These murders were not
rumors; unbelievably enough, they took place only fifty
years ago.

The berserk whites even attempted lynchings, several
of which were successful. The explanation was made that
"Southern niggers deserve a genuine lynching." A reporter described the hanging of a Negro whose head had
been smashed open by clubs and who lay bloody, unconscious, and near death:

"I saw the most sickening incident of the evening when
they got stronger rope. To put the rope around the Negro's
neck, one of the lynchers stuck his fingers inside the
gaping scalp and lifted the Negro's head by it, literally
bathing his hand in the man's blood. 'Get hold, and pull
for East St. Louis,' called the man as he seized the other
end of the rope. The Negro was lifted to a height of about
seven feet and the body left hanging there for hours."

More soldiers arrived during the evening, and in many
cases the activities of the rioters were restrained by their
presence. On the other hand, abundant later testimony
indicated that the guardsmen often participated in the
attacks rather than preventing them. One of the deplorable
aspects of the riot was that the majority of both local
policemen and the Illinois guardsmen were sympathetic to
the rioters, and several times they refused pleas for help
or actually shot Negroes for no apparent reason other
than their own bias.

The burning continued throughout the night and the
flames could be seen many miles away. The toll for the
evening was more than two hundred houses reduced to
ashes in a completely burned-out, sixteen-block area. The

official figure for buildings totally destroyed during the
twenty-four hours was 312.

As in almost all riots, the immediate reports of casualties
were grossly exaggerated. Blazing headlines throughout
the United States gave the number of Negro dead as from
one hundred to four hundred. The front page of the St.
Louis *Globe-Democrat* of July 3 was topped by the bold
letters "100 NEGROES SHOT, BURNED, CLUBBED TO DEATH IN
E. ST. LOUIS RACE WAR." The East St. Louis police department estimated an official figure (both Negroes and
whites) as one hundred. The congressional investigating
committee indicated that an exact figure was impossible
to determine, but fixed the toll of dead as eight whites
and thirty-nine Negroes. Hundreds of Negroes were
wounded and hundreds left the city never to return.

The riot was studied in detail in three special investigations—a local St. Clair County grand jury, a board of
inquiry of the Illinois National Guard, and a special committee of the United States House of Representatives. The
published versions of the hearings, however, were abridged
and therefore appear to have omitted unpleasant testimony.

The state's attorney in St. Clair County claimed that
he could prosecute no one because he was unable to find
a single person who witnessed any citizens committing
violence on July 2!

Nevertheless a grand jury drew up indictments against
eighty-two whites and twenty-three Negroes. Trials on
charges of assault with intent to murder and conspiracy
to riot resulted in twenty-one prison sentences—nine
whites and twelve Negroes. This was admittedly a some-

what puzzling situation, since only four of the imprisoned
whites were tried for homicide (murder) though thirty-
nine Negroes were murdered, while eleven of the Negroes
were sentenced for the killing of the two detectives. The
light penalties of whites who pleaded guilty to lesser
charges were imposed without trials, since no witnesses
came forth to testify. Thus Negroes continued to be the
victims of discrimination even in the law courts.

In the court of public opinion and in the congressional
investigation, East St. Louis and its riotous citizens were
strongly condemned. The city government, the employers,
the labor organizers, and the politicians were charged with
the conditions which produced the riot. The machinations
of political power and the open partiality of the law, from
detention and arrest to trial, were openly exposed.

The number of race riots before the present century has
never been completely established. But when the American
Negro attempted to find his place in an overwhelmingly
white society, clashes became inevitable. In a study of
racial tensions, Professor Allen Grimshaw of Indiana
University identifies thirty-three "major interracial disturbances" in the United States between 1900 and 1949.
Eighteen of these occurred between 1915 and 1919, the
period of the First World War. Five major riots took
place between 1940 and 1944, but only one (Detroit in
1943) was as violent as those of the previous period. Dr.
Grimshaw's study does not include the 1950s and 1960s
with their serious race riots.

At least two other race riots, though not matching it,
approached that of East St. Louis in scope and ferocity.
In Chicago a thirteen-day riot in July 1919 took a toll

of 38 persons killed (15 whites and 23 Negroes), 537 injured (178 whites, 342 Negroes, and 17 of unidentified race). More than a thousand families, mostly Negroes, were left without homes as a result of burning or destruction. The riot began when a Negro swimmer drifted into the water of a segregated beach.

A third major riot was that in Detroit in June 1943, where 25 Negroes and 9 whites died and at least 700 persons were injured. This outbreak began with a fist fight between a white man and a Negro.

Most of the race riots in Northern cities through the 1940s resulted from identical underlying causes, according to Dr. Grimshaw: "threats to the security of whites brought on by the Negroes' gains in economic, political, and social status; Negro resentment of the attempts to 'kick him back into his place'; and the weakness of the local city government, particularly the police department."

POLICE STRIKE
Boston
September 9-12, 1919

Invitation to Lawlessness

AT THE routine 5:45 P.M. roll call following the day shift on Tuesday, September 9, 1919, slightly more than eleven hundred of the 1450 patrolmen on the Boston police force answered "Not present" when their names were called. They turned in their badges, revolvers, billy clubs, and locker keys to their precinct captains and walked out of the nineteen district station houses throughout the city. The name of each departing patrolman was noted on the roster as "Absent without leave."

The policemen of The Hub were going out on strike.

This exodus, not at all unforeseen, was an almost open invitation to mischief, thievery, and every sort of crime. The 750,000 citizens of Boston lacked the basis of all city police protection, the everyday security of the cop on the beat. No major American metropolis had ever before been so unprotected.

The strike was no surprise, for all citizens were familiar with the grievances of the patrolmen. The pay was low at a time when the wartime economy was booming. The station houses were run down, unsanitary, and crowded. Promotion was based on favoritism rather than merit or civil service examinations. The pension scheme was woefully inadequate.

The policemen had reached the end of their patience. Police Commissioner Edwin Curtis, an aristocrat and former mayor of Boston, considered them nagging troublemakers. To him their protests represented rebellion.

Feeling that an alliance with the American Federation of Labor would aid them in pressing their demands, the patrolmen had already formed a union local and elected eight officers in mid-August. Commissioner Curtis belatedly forbade his men to join, tried the union officers for disobedience and, since he was the sole judge, found them guilty. He then filed charges against eleven other leaders. All the sentences were to be announced on September 4. The union immediately threatened a strike if the nineteen were discharged from the force.

As middleman, Mayor Andrew Peters set up a committee of citizens to arbitrate the dispute. Their appeal to Governor Calvin Coolidge, who had appointed Curtis, to interfere was abruptly refused.

On Monday afternoon, September 8, the commissioner suspended the nineteen men for disobeying his order, and that night the union members unanimously voted to strike on the next afternoon.

Bostonians spent Tuesday frantically preparing for the unknown future. Stores, business firms, and banks organized special protective forces. Several hundred citizen volunteers, including the entire Harvard football team, were deputized as policemen. The Metropolitan Park Police force of a hundred was called for special city duty. The city awaited the fateful hour.

At three of the nineteen stations the entire force walked out; the average number leaving the others was ninety per cent. Word of the walkout spread rapidly in the haunts of the lawless throughout the city. This was a once-in-a-lifetime opportunity.

Thousands of shops and businesses were unprotected. Only the plate-glass windows separated the displayed goods from those who wished to possess them. The selection was endless. Since prices were at an all-time war level, making the resale price high, even undreamed of luxuries were within reach.

Juvenile troublemakers were the first to test the situation in outbreaks of vandalism, such as pulling trolleys from their overhead wires and smashing car windows. When no policemen arrived, they grew bolder and more destructive, stealing automobiles, stripping and then abandoning them. They piled boxes on the streetcar tracks and stoned passengers fleeing from the stalled cars. They turned in scores of false fire alarms. It was all great fun.

The small number of available non-striking policemen and officers remained in the various station houses with the members of the Metropolitan Park Police force; these men had been assigned to the stations from which the largest number of patrolmen had walked out. The volunteer enrollees were on call. No policeman was to venture out on the streets unless there was a serious emergency. Not a single patrolman was walking his beat.

The way was now clear for more full-scale lawlessness, which erupted almost simultaneously in two widely separated sections of the city.

Near the downtown business area, ruffians had been collecting in Scollay Square, an area of honky-tonks, cheap bars, burlesque and all-night movie theaters, flophouses, penny arcades, and shooting galleries. Scollay Square was within a block of the courthouse police station, where only ten of the normal force of 129 were on duty, and almost within the shadow of City Hall and the central police headquarters.

Minute by minute the square had filled up. By 10:30 P.M. about five thousand people had collected there, milling around as if waiting for someone or some act to send them into action.

Late in the evening a roaming gang of boys swept into a nearby burlesque theater and stopped the performance with their yelling and shouting before being thrown out by the bouncers.

This group, joined by a large number of idlers, immediately began smashing the plate-glass windows of an adjoining shoe store. A few boys calmly stepped through and began handing out the shoes in the display and clearing the shelves of their boxes. This successful and effortless robbery was the spark that ignited the flame of wild and wanton destruction and plunder.

Nearby, all along Hanover Street the ever swelling, jubilant crowds smashed store windows, loading their arms with shoes, haberdashery, and clothing. Turning on Washington Street, this group moved rapidly toward the wholesale market district, storming the many provision stores in the vicinity, loading themselves with every kind of fruit and vegetable as they swept tumultuously along the streets. They dispersed only when the watchman of a warehouse stood them off for twenty minutes by calmly aiming his .38-caliber revolver and daring any one of their number to advance.

At Haymarket Square, these first rioters found others ready and eager to unite with them. At the cry "Come on!" they accomplished their first large-scale looting by cleaning out the stocks of both a cigar and a clothing store. But soon six police sergeants arrived, charged with revolvers, and momentarily scattered them.

The thrill of vandalism had seized and invigorated the mob; they were intoxicated by their success. Sizable crowds now covered all the crooked streets and narrow alleys of this older section of Boston. The small units of police and volunteers dispatched from time to time could only play a game of hide-and-seek in the maze of streets. When they met a group and sent them on the run, the determined rioters merely reassembled elsewhere.

Plundering crowds were soon operating everywhere throughout the area. Oblivious to the surrounding turmoil, drunken men played crap games in the middle of the street, completely blocking it.

The infection of vandalism spread rapidly, and the main concentration of downtown retail shops and department stores farther down Washington Street, the main business thoroughfare, fell victims to the mob. The large department stores such as Filene's, Jordan Marsh, and R. H. White's, were spared only because scores of armed watchmen stood at the entrances. Instead, two or three dozen smaller shops of all types received the crowd's attention. Men laden with shirts, neckties, and jewelry brazenly walked along Washington Street, openly trading their loot. Fifteen of the shoe stores along the route were completely pillaged. Plunderers helped each other to find pairs of the proper size; robbers sat calmly on the curbstones trying them on.

The crowd moved rapidly from store to store on both sides of the street, and few establishments were spared. The broken show-window glass was inches deep in places.

From time to time a small roving unit of police inspectors and officers sped up in a truck or car, fired a few shots into the air, and succeeded in scattering the turbulent crowd. The rioters would run down the side streets, only to gather again in strength on Washington Street a few minutes later.

The Washington Street mob streamed past the Adams House where Governor Coolidge was sleeping peacefully on an upper floor. Like many other Bostonians, he was to read of the disturbances in the morning papers.

A part of the emboldened crowd had already turned on the side streets, continuing to loot the stores as they moved toward Tremont Street. The stores on this street opposite the Common were among the most exclusive in Boston. Many a poor Boston woman of limited means was later clothed in the expensive dresses, furs, hats, and jewels from these stores.

Boston Common was a pride of the city. But now, under the lights along the mall, which ran the full length of its east side, scores of crap games were in progress. Knots of men shot dice without interference, and many a player was relieved of his winnings by waiting thugs as he left the game.

Boston had never seen such a bold display of lawlessness, such open defiance of its statutes, as on this Tuesday night. For more than two hours the downtown area seethed with robbery and looting. The few available police units were almost completely ineffective against the widespread destruction.

At midnight the Provost Guard was summoned from the Charlestown Navy Yard across the bay to support the police. At one o'clock on Wednesday morning the police asked the Edison Company to keep all street lights burning until daylight.

Scenes of even greater violence were being simultaneously played out in South Boston, a slum area near the busy waterfront. Its citizens lived in shabby tenements, hovels, flats, cheap hotels, and boarding houses. The section was the gathering place for dockworkers, stevedores, low-paid laborers, petty and hardened criminals, thieves, pickpockets, and gamblers. Hundreds of bars and saloons lined the streets.

The principal thoroughfare was West Broadway, the long blocks of which were intersected by six main streets alphabetically labeled from A through F, with Dorchester Avenue at one end and Dorchester Street at the other.

On Tuesday evening only twenty men were on duty at one of the two police stations; the other was manned by a few officers and Metropolitan Park Police.

Trouble began when a throng of about fifteen hundred gathered at the D Street station, waiting for the men to leave their posts at 5:45 P.M. Within an hour the mob had increased to five thousand.

A mob had gathered in full strength the entire length of West Broadway from B to Dorchester streets. Ten available non-striking patrolmen spaced themselves at intervals along the curbstones near D Street where the largest numbers had gathered. Trouble immediately broke out on both sides of the little company of impotent policemen, and rowdies began cutting a swath along several blocks of West Broadway, smashing the windows of more than two dozen stores and running off with the contents. Markets, haberdasheries, variety, and shoe stores were completely cleaned out. All this was within a block on each side of the police, who could not penetrate the barriers formed by the mob. Scores of plate-glass windows were broken. The sidewalks and streets were soon carpeted with fragments of the shattered glass. Though shopowners fired revolvers over the heads of the crowd, the depredations continued.

At two huge markets the leaders of the robbers handed out eggs by the crate. Rowdies enjoyed a free-for-all, pelting everyone in sight. The superintendent of police arrived from downtown Boston with a few patrolmen and brought an end to the disturbance.

By eleven o'clock West Broadway and its intersecting streets were black with a noisy, tumultuous crowd which had increased to eight thousand, all actively looting. A few available police formed at intervals along Broadway but could make no headway against the milling, shouting, and hooting rabble who pelted them with refuse, mud, and rocks.

Stores in two entire blocks along West Broadway suddenly became the objects of attack—a Woolworth five-and-ten-cent store, six shoe stores, a dozen dry-goods and clothing stores, tailor shops, four groceries, three bakeries, and saloons and liquor stores. There was enough for everybody; no one waited to make a selection but snatched the first items within reach.

On Dorchester Avenue, to the southwest, a similar reign of terror was taking place. A crowd of several thousand filled the street from curb to curb, overflowing into the side streets. Looting of stores along the avenue began. With bricks and paving blocks the robbers attacked the few policemen sent to quell the disturbance. But the officers, their revolvers in one hand and clubs in the other, walked fearlessly into the crowds. This surprising show of force cowed the drunken and savage mob.

In the face of the continued opposition, the outnumbered regular and volunteer police in South Boston could only discharge their revolvers and hurry back to the security of the station houses. Whole sections of South Boston were completely devastated as if a tornado had struck. The rioters were in full and undisputed possession. For two or three hours they robbed with little interference.

Only a few scattered outbreaks erupted in other sections of the city. Peace and quiet had prevailed throughout the greater part of Boston.

As if on signal, early Wednesday morning the uprising gradually ceased. The night of violence was at last at an end.

Citizens read the headlines in Wednesday morning's newspapers with both disbelief and horror. The head of the policemen's union stoutly maintained that the responsibility for the evening's rioting and looting rested with Commissioner Curtis, not with the striking policemen, that advance notice of the walkout had been given and the public had been told that an emergency force was available.

Tuesday night's destruction served notice that the mob would only wait until darkness to reassemble. The city was feverish with activity and suspense. The mayor forbade the sale of firearms. Storekeepers boarded up their show windows, often stringing barbed wire over the entrances.

Mayor Peters began to act late on Wednesday morning. He called out the State Guard units stationed in the city, totaling a thousand, and ordered them to be ready for service at five o'clock. Then he took command of the Police Department and asked Governor Coolidge for an additional three thousand guardsmen. By darkness the city was an armed camp. The metropolis was ablaze on Wednesday night. Steel-helmeted guardsmen were being rushed everywhere throughout the city. Armed watchmen were in most buildings and stores. The volunteer police were assigned to major spots where trouble might again be anticipated.

Cavalry units of the State Guard now patrolled Scollay Square, riding their horses on the sidewalks and forcing the crowd to keep moving. This crowd of five thousand refused to disperse. Early in the evening pistol shots rang out and the horsemen made a bayonet charge, driving the mob into the side streets. The crowd stampeded like cattle. Men and women attempting to escape fell over each other, trampling those who stumbled and fell. Those on the sidewalks were pushed against the glass store windows which shattered at the pressure, cutting many. Pickpockets took advantage of the confusion to ply their skills.

Shots whistled through the air. Men on roofs hurled rocks upon the cavalrymen and the crowds filling the narrow streets. When a man in the throng fell dead from a shot fired from above, the mob seemed momentarily sobered.

But by nine o'clock Scollay Square was again packed solidly with human beings. The rioters set up a barrage of bottles, mud, paving stones, and brickbats. Missiles rained from the rooftops. Infantry reinforcements finally charged the throng with drawn bayonets, cleared the square, and posted sentinels along the cross streets.

Remnants of the mob now surged through the side streets, repeating the attacks of Tuesday night on stores, more than forty of which were completely sacked.

The soldiers broke up dice games in Avery Street and again on the Common. By midnight guardsmen were stationed at intervals of twenty feet on both sides of Washington Street. Downtown Boston was under control.

South Boston had erupted again on Wednesday night. A crowd of five thousand gathered along West Broadway, doubling within an hour to number ten thousand, the largest of any during the strike. This mob decided to test its strength against the show of opposition.

Armed gangs went on a rampage. Another dozen stores were broken into and wiped out in the well-established pattern.

By ten o'clock the crowd, now considerably decreased in numbers, became bolder. Enraged by the soldiers' rifles and bared bayonets on the street, some of the more daring took places in windows on the upper floors and began shooting at the perfect targets presented by the soldiers standing at attention below.

The moment of decision came toward midnight. The guardsmen poured volley after volley of gunfire directly into the packed crowd, which scattered in all directions. When the smoke cleared two men were dead and nine persons (six men and three women) lay seriously injured in the street. A third man died later. But control was established.

Stores were still being robbed in other parts of Boston. Hundreds of holdups were reported. But order had been restored by early Thursday morning.

The riot had now received national attention. In an address at Helena, Montana, President Woodrow Wilson said, "A strike of policemen in a great city, leaving that city at the mercy of thugs, is a crime against civilization."

Fresh troops with fixed bayonets, ammunition in their belts and rifles, immediately established the power of law and order. Scollay Square and South Boston were now fully protected. When the dice games began again on the Common the soldiers shot directly at the players, killing one. Forty men were arrested.

Governor Coolidge was forced to take belated action on Thursday morning. He called out the State Guard units from other parts of Massachusetts to maintain order.

Commissioner Curtis declared the posts of all the striking patrolmen vacant, thus dismissing them, and began rebuilding his force. He now belatedly considered the complaints of the ex-patrolmen and planned to introduce changes. When President Samuel Gompers of the American Federation of Labor urged that they be reinstated,

Coolidge made the fourteen-word statement that brought him national prominence and eventually led him to the White House: "There is no right to strike against the public safety by anybody, any time, anywhere."

During the uprising nine rioters had been killed and fifty-eight wounded, twenty-three seriously. At its peak strength Guard units numbering seventy-five hundred were on duty in the city, and the last did not leave until just before Christmas.

The mob violence during the Boston police strike was unique among American riots. The rioters had no particular sympathy with the strikers; they simply took advantage of the situation to indulge in extensive robbery, looting, and destruction. Never before or since has a mob been given the opportunity to take over a large American city which lacked police protection.

As of 1962, eleven states had no-strike laws applying to public employees. Action forbidding United States civil service employees to strike was taken by the 84th Congress in 1955. Public Law 330 (U. S. Code, Section 118 P-R, 1958) makes it a felony punishable by up to a fine of a thousand dollars and a year and a day in jail for federal employees who strike "or assert the right to strike or knowingly belong to an organization that does."

13

```
THE BONUS ARMY
Washington, D. C.
July 28, 1932
```

The Tenacity of Desperate Men

THE MARCH as a form of protest has been one of the main weapons of the nonviolent Negro civil rights movement. The March on Washington for Jobs and Freedom on August 28, 1963, in the hundredth year after the Emancipation Proclamation, was an unforgettable example of peaceable demonstration; it was well planned, orderly, and dignified.

Protest marches are nothing new to our nation's capital. Marches by Americans on the city that houses their government stem from historic rights, rights contained in the First Amendment to the Constitution. The amendment forbids Congress to make any law that abridges "the right of the people peaceably to assemble, and to petition the government for a redress of grievances." These marches have been undertaken for all kinds of reasons. The marchers at times have been welcomed; at other times they have been met with hostility, scorn, arrest, and even death.

The most notable protest of the nineteenth century

was the march of "Coxey's Army" on Washington in 1894.
The year was one of deep depression; strikes were numerous (see Chapter 9, Pullman Strike), wages were low
and unemployment high. Jacob Coxey of Massillon, Ohio,
decided to lead the unemployed of his town to the capital
to demand non-interest-bearing government loans to states
and cities for public works (at that time an unprecedented
suggestion). About four hundred finally reached Washington. When Coxey was refused a permit to demonstrate, he
and a small group went to the steps of the Capitol on
May 1. Washington mounted police charged the group
and arrested them for trespassing. "General" Coxey was
fined five dollars and spent twenty days in jail. The government eventually offered the "army" free transportation
home.

The great postwar depression began in 1929 with the
stock market crash which affected banking, commerce,
and industry. The rise in production costs and lessened
demand forced curtailment of production, the dismissal
of employees, or wage cuts. By 1932 the number of unemployed had risen to ten million. The Republican administration of President Herbert Hoover opposed direct
federal relief to individuals and substituted work programs. Even so, the situation of the unemployed was
desperate.

A bonus for World War I veterans had been voted in
1924, to be paid in the form of twenty-year endowment
policies on which ex-servicemen might borrow from the
government up to about twenty-five per cent of full value.
However, no cash payments were to be made. As the

depression deepened, veterans' groups demanded immediate enactment of a bill raising the borrowing limit to fifty per cent. Congress passed such a bill, but President Hoover vetoed it in February 1931. Congress then passed the bill over his veto. Later in the year Democratic leaders proposed that the entire bonus be paid immediately in cash both to bolster the economy and to aid the unemployed veterans.

This demand for the immediate cashing of the bonus certificates in full provided the impetus behind the 1932 Bonus March, while Congress was debating the Patman bill calling for payment of $2,400,000,000. The march began under the leadership of an unemployed cannery worker in Portland, Oregon, from which three hundred veterans (with less than thirty dollars among them) began the transcontinental journey which was to take eighteen days, some riding freight cars, others in trucks supplied by each state through which they crossed. Veterans from other states began the trek. Those from Minnesota came in boxcars, nine hundred from Cleveland seized trains in the local railroad yard. By the first week in June twenty thousand veterans, many with their families, were in Washington.

The District of Columbia authorities aided them in securing food and shelter. The government building program on Pennsylvania Avenue not far from the Capitol was halted in order to house some of the marchers in a number of partially razed temporary buildings of the Treasury Department which had been erected for use during World War I. The main camp was located across the Anacostia River where, in addition to army tents, hundreds of shacks were erected from all sorts of materials. Egg crates, junked autos, bed frames, barrels filled with hay, and even a piano box and an empty coffin served as shelter. Food was supplied from limited available relief funds.

Each day thousands of the Bonus Army (the official name selected was the Bonus Expeditionary Force, which issued a daily newspaper) packed the steps of an area surrounding the Capitol. Groups openly lobbied with and pressured their congressmen; parades were everywhere, soapbox orators enjoyed a field day. Except for the annoyance caused by their presence, the marchers were peaceful. Some of the congressmen recklessly made promises and raised the hopes of the Army.

The House passed the Patman (Bonus) bill on June 15. The President, however, announced that he would veto it, and two nights later, with twelve thousand veterans tensely milling about the Capitol, the Senate rejected the measure by an overwhelming vote. Before adjourning the next day, Congress appropriated a hundred thousand dollars to transport the veterans to their homes. The money was to be a non-interest loan to be charged against the final individual bonus payment. Many left the capital, only to be replaced by new arrivals.

During June and early July all was quiet. But such a frustrated and discontented crowd was soon to become more active, and demonstrations became daily occurrences. Attempts to picket the White House were broken up by District police. The more radical element, a hard core of known Communist Party members, began to encourage open hostility in place of the peaceful demonstrations which had accomplished nothing. By late July about six thousand of the B.E.F. had left, but seven thousand still remained.

The patience of government officials had meanwhile been sorely tried. The veterans had outlasted their welcome. The Treasury authorities were eager to resume work on the buildings undergoing demolition. They asked that protection be given their agents in the task of repossessing the skeleton structures. Police Chief Pelham D. Glassford, a retired army general, was instructed to furnish police protection. To give adequate notice to the two hundred veteran occupants, a formal notice to vacate was posted on the twenty-third. The date set was Thursday, July 28.

Late that morning the Treasury employees arrived with a guard of about a hundred police. The evacuation was quickly completed without incident by 11:50 A.M. But observers from nearby camps were dissatisfied with such an "abject surrender."

These were the Communists who had instigated the more vocal and disorderly demonstrations and parades. At the sight of their fellow veterans' peaceful compliance with what they considered an unreasonable order, they resorted to the violence and resistance which later testimony revealed had been their purpose in infiltrating the Bonus Army. The result was two separate incidents which were undoubtedly the shortest riots on record.

A few minutes after noon about fifty of these malcontents, carrying an American flag, formed a wedge and attacked a line of police, pelting them with showers of bricks from the numerous piles surrounding the partially

demolished buildings. Some of the rioters used pieces of
lumber, scraps of iron, and rocks. Within five minutes
the police, by using their billy clubs freely, had subdued
their attackers and dispersed them.

But no mob, however small, is content to accept defeat
as long as continued resistance is possible. The story
behind the second attack, which occurred at 1:45 P.M.,
has never been completely revealed, but the radical
leaders apparently ordered another attack on the forces
of law. Some of these troublemakers urged several of those
evicted to recover their lost quarters. As they mounted a
stairway to the second floor where four police stood on
guard they began to curse and threaten two of the officers,
forcing them into a corner. Since there was no doubt that
they were in serious physical danger, the policemen drew
their pistols and fired half a dozen shots at their tor-
mentors. Whether they fired just before the assault or
whether they were knocked down and fired while on their
knees is not certain. One veteran was killed instantly, a
second wounded fatally. Three injured policemen were
taken to the hospital. The riot was over.

The District of Columbia officials had asked President
Hoover for federal troops after the first outbreak. Since
the District was government territory it was not necessary
to proclaim martial law. At about three o'clock Secretary
of War Patrick J. Hurley gave an order to the army Chief
of Staff, General Douglas MacArthur: "You will have
United States troops proceed immediately to the scene
of the disorder. Surround the affected area and clear it
without delay. . . . Use all humanity consistent with the
due execution of this order."

Almost immediately a column of infantry and cavalry

with five tanks in support converged on the partially demolished buildings. This was a military operation, and there was not a life lost or a single serious injury. About five hundred soldiers had assembled at the scene by 5 P.M. After half an hour's wait the troops donned gas masks and in a few minutes of tear-gas bombing completely cleared the area. Though no shots were fired there was a considerable display of swinging cavalry sabers and prodding bayonets. This incident was *not* a riot, though many sympathetic and emotional accounts sought to present the operation as such. By nine o'clock the clearing operation had been completed and the vacated billets burned.

The soldiers next completed the destruction of the Anacostia Camp, with its makeshift shelters and tents, after all the veterans and their families had been told to leave. Flames lit up the midnight sky and the stunned remnants of the Bonus Expeditionary Force made their way to Maryland, then into Pennsylvania, and finally filtered back to their homes, wretched victims of their lost cause.

The World War I veterans' bonus measure was finally passed in 1936 during the Roosevelt administration. It was intended to bolster the post-depression economy.

The Bonus Army highlighted a concept which had begun with pension payments to Civil War veterans—that civilians drafted into compulsory military service were entitled to a special compensation later. Veterans' benefits now form a substantial part of the national budget.

14

PRISON RIOT

Jackson, Mich.

April 20-24, 1952

Outbreak Behind Bars

OF ALL types, prison riots are the most familiar. On film and television we have over and over again seen the rebellious hardened inmate of "the big house" as the strong leader who plans pressure against the authorities to correct a condition or obtain new privileges. The pattern of the actual riot seldom varies—the keys to the cell block are seized, guards ("screws") are held as hostages, threats are made, shots may be fired or tear gas used, and bargaining begins. The outbreak may spread throughout the entire prison, with incidents of violence. Promises may or may not be made, a truce is finally declared, and the riot is finished.

The unique character of the prison population lends itself to violent outbreaks. Confinement causes both psychological and physical pressures which very often can be relieved only by "blowing off steam." An inmate has seemingly endless hours to nourish his resentment against society and authority. If he is a leader he will have no difficulty in recruiting fellow conspirators, and the riot plan becomes a reality.

Penologists assert that prisoners dislike a strike or riot, since it leads to restricted privileges and tightened discipline. However, once a disorder begins, the inmates invariably participate, for the approval of others is not only desirable but necessary.

Prison disorders are generally led by a small group of violently unstable men who respect only strict discipline and misinterpret lenience and kindness as weaknesses. These leaders are termed "hard-core" prisoners, those who openly resent the restrictions of their lives and who bolster their self-importance by gathering the weak around them as followers.

During the eighteen months between April 1952 and September 1953, thirty major prison riots erupted in a "chain" throughout the United States; this was more than in the previous twenty-five years. Penologist Paul Tappan has expressed the opinion that appeasement of rioting inmates in some penal institutions stimulated riots in others. "The discovery that threats, violence, and destruction may gain concessions," he stated, "has had anomalous consequences."

These riots occurred in all parts of the country—California, Idaho, Illinois, Kentucky, Louisiana, Massachusetts, Michigan, New Jersey, New Mexico, North Carolina, Ohio, and Utah—and were of all sizes and types. None involved attempts at mass escapes, but the purpose of each was apparently to call public attention to undesirable conditions of prison life.

The riot pattern was the same in all prisons: hostages were seized; the prisoners barricaded themselves; all available property was destroyed; and demands, followed by "bargaining," were made on all the prison or political officials of the state. These formal demands were for better food, better medical care, better recreational facilities, less rigid disciplinary rules, and more liberal parole practices.

The largest in this wave of riots was the five-day siege at Southern Michigan Prison in Jackson, seventy-five miles west of Detroit, from April 20-24, 1952. In terms of damage and the number of convicts involved the Jackson riot was the biggest in United States prison history.

The Jackson institution was at the time the largest walled prison in the country, with space allotted for 4,827. But in 1952 the prison population was 6,490 convicts. This riot has become the classic example of its type, for it followed the oft-repeated, typical pattern to perfection.

The explosion on Sunday evening, April 20, began in Cell Block 15, the detention block for unruly prisoners, those disciplinary problems who are too dangerous to remain with other inmates and must be temporarily or permanently isolated for the general good. At that time there were 185 men in the five-story oblong brick building. Forty-three were in solitary confinement cells (called The Hole), the remainder in single "segregation" cells. In such a situation the tough, dangerous men become the leaders. Earl Ward, a repeater with a long record, and "Crazy" Jack Hyatt, who had once attempted to escape from another Michigan prison by using visiting Governor G. Mennen Williams as a shield, commanded this outbreak.

After the 15-Block inmates had returned from dinner and all was quiet, a convict tricked a new and inexperienced guard into unlocking his cell door. He then seized the keys, locked the guard in, and released Ward and Hyatt. The riot had commenced.

Armed with knives (the usual inspection had been omitted that evening), the three soon seized the four duty guards, locked them into cells, and systematically released every one of the block's prisoners on the five floors. In a frenzy of freedom they smashed everything in sight, stole razors from the barbershop, and wandered through the corridors without any definite purpose or plan of action. Without being either elected or requested, Earl Ward took charge. He notified the guard chief by telephone of the situation in Block 15. He demanded an interview with the warden. Then he requested that the block's doors be locked. Soon he asked to talk with a reporter, and in the subsequent interview complained of guard brutality. A swarm of other newsmen were granted interviews at midnight and one of the captive guards was brought out by Ward to talk to them. Prison officials could make no progress in negotiations for the release of the hostages.

News of the mutiny spread rapidly throughout the other twelve cell blocks, each of which housed about five hundred men. Early on Monday morning half the inmates breakfasted in the mess hall and returned to their blocks, but when the second shift was settling down one man yelled and threw his tray into the air. Bedlam followed. The central yard soon filled up. Those in the mess hall began a systematic plunder of the kitchens, then the commissary. From the butchers' tables they seized knives, choppers, and cleavers, from the shops tools, hammers, and iron bars. They burned the laundry, the library, the greenhouse, and the chapel. They plundered the supply rooms. "It was a seething mob of people running in all directions, yelling and screaming, dashing past like maniacs," an inmate later said, "all pillaging, burning, wrecking, and looting." The riot in Cell Block 15 had become a general prison riot.

Ward was soon in command of this riot. Other guards, some beaten, wounded, and bleeding, were brought to 15-Block until the number held was thirteen. Half the prison population, about twenty-five hundred, were entering all the cell blocks, releasing their occupants, smashing everything possible. The floors of some of the buildings were ankle-deep in water, broken glass, and wreckage. Fist fights to settle long-smoldering disputes and enmities were taking place everywhere. The noise and clamor were deafening. Smoke filled the air. Some of the inmates refused to participate and watched the wild spectacle in disbelief. "My friends looked like wild men," a nonparticipant recalled. "I saw boys that I know and never thought would do violence," he continued, "with their hair hanging down and bloodshot eyes. I seen the look on some of the guys, and they seemed like they'd gone crazy."

The state police had been alerted the night before and now they were desperately needed. At about ten-thirty some two hundred troopers arrived carrying sawed-off shotguns, rifles, sidearms, and tear-gas guns. In each block they herded the convicts into cells and, when possible, locked the doors. Then they wiped out scattered pockets of resistance before attacking the main body in the yard. A convict who refused to move was shot dead. The troopers advanced in a spread-out line, guns at ready. The rioters moved slowly and deliberately, but some sat down on the ground and refused to get up until prodded by guns or frightened by shots fired over their heads. To

speed the clearing process the troopers fired their gas
guns and this encouraged the choking convicts to move.
When the rioters staged a second sit-down the soldiers
fired more directly and wounded three convicts.

The yard was finally cleared. All the prisoners were in
their blocks, though not in their cells, for one of the most
popular activities had been the smashing of thousands of
locks. For the rest of the day they ran unrestrained on all
the cell levels, screaming and smashing whatever had
been overlooked. Finally troopers kept the men in their
cells by making regular circuits of each floor with drawn
pistols, at the same time inspecting the cells and throwing
debris down to the main-floor level. Starting at five
o'clock, the convicts, who had had no lunch, were fed in
their cells, since sending them to the mess hall involved
too great a risk. The last convict was fed at midnight.

The prison was quiet. The general riot was over. One
convict was dead, nine wounded, and $2,500,000 worth of
prison property had been smashed and burned.

But Ward and Hyatt still remained in the wrecked Cell
Block 15, holding twelve guards as hostages on the top
floor (one had been turned loose to the mercy of the yard
mob but had been almost miraculously rescued by the
troopers). Storming the building to free them appeared too
dangerous. Negotiation appeared to be the only sensible
course of action.

On Tuesday morning the deputy warden began bargaining with ringleader Earl Ward for terms of surrender. For
two days Ward presented his demands, occasionally releasing a guard in token of his good faith. An eleven-point
agreement was settled upon, but Ward delayed approval
until he had received newspaper and radio publicity, for

he considered himself a victorious and heroic leader. The most outrageous demand was that no reprisals should be taken against the rioters.

On Thursday afternoon at four o'clock the prisoners in Cell Block 15 surrendered. The eight remaining hostages were released and the inmates marched to the mess hall for a victory banquet (with photographers, newsmen, and radio broadcasters as special guests), including steak and ice cream which Ward had ordered specially.

Months passed before the damage was repaired. The riot leaders, including Ward and Hyatt, were scattered among other state institutions. Official and unofficial investigations produced recommendations for improvements which would eliminate further possible riots. The new warden, a strict disciplinarian, organized a riot squad which took the place of the state police, who left on Labor Day. They had meanwhile stopped a full-scale riot, with guards seized as hostages, in one of the cell blocks by the simple expedient of shooting. In November another riot began in the mess hall, but this time the riot squad used their machine guns and peace was restored.

The rash of 1952 riots resulted in several conferences and studies examining the common causes and complaints. Some attempts were made to correct the bad conditions. Additional appropriations permitted new construction in at least three of the states involved to correct the complaint of overcrowding.

"Prisoner committees" are now commonly accepted as good practice. They represent the inmates in discussions with administrative officers.

15

THE NEGRO CIVIL RIGHTS MOVEMENT
1954-1965

"We Shall Overcome"

THE APPALLING number of race riots of whites against Negroes in the first two decades of the present century, as cited in Chapter 11, is conclusive proof of the oppression of the Negro in both North and South during and after World War I, when for the first time the man of color became a threat to the economic security of the established white workers. This competition resulted in the peak number of twenty-six race riots in American cities during 1919.

Negroes who had moved to the urban industrial areas of the North found many of the very conditions they had hoped to leave behind them. Segregation in housing, discrimination in employment opportunities, and often, because of segregation, inferior schools for their children, proved to be barriers to the attainment of the good life for which they had hoped.

The Southern Negroes continued to be completely second-class citizens in a menial condition. An additional deprivation was of the right to vote; with only a few local exceptions Negroes in the South were disfranchised.

For the past half century two national organizations have been active in working toward gaining full equality for the Negro as an American citizen—the National Association for the Advancement of Colored People (NAACP), founded in 1909, and the National Urban League, formed in 1911. The NAACP has always emphasized the protection of Negro rights through legal means. Most of the local and national legislation for the improvement of the race in the last fifty years has been sponsored by the organization, and the decrease in Negro lynchings is credited to its sponsorship of anti-lynching legislation. All types of discrimination—in education, in voting rights, in housing, and in work—received continuous NAACP attention through the years preceding the federal civil rights legislation of the late 1950s and early 1960s. The Association sponsored and fought to the U. S. Supreme Court the case (Brown vs. Board of Education of Topeka, Kansas) which made segregated schools illegal, the first landmark in the current civil rights movement. Since this 1954 decision the NAACP, through its Legal Defense and Education Fund, has undertaken and underwritten court cases.

The National Urban League, as its name implies, works through its many branches to improve the employment opportunities of Negroes in cities and industrial areas.

Local branches of the NAACP and the National Urban League have participated in the action programs of the current movements (demonstrations), though the League, which had sponsored Negro protests in the North, withdrew in 1964. In the Southern states the majority of the protest activities have been sponsored by the Rev. Martin

Luther King, Jr.'s nonviolent Southern Christian Leadership Conference and the two more militant Negro organizations, the Congress of Racial Equality (CORE) and the Student Nonviolent Coordinating Committee (SNCC). All these organizations have biracial memberships.

The contemporary civil rights drive may be said to have been accelerated when federal action was taken on school segregation. In a sweeping and unanimous decision on May 17, 1954, the United States Supreme Court ruled that racial segregation in public schools is unconstitutional, that separate educational facilities are "inherently unequal." The latter struck at the "separate but equal" doctrine in the South, with its inferior facilities and teaching. This momentous decision affected twenty-one states —seventeen of which at that time required segregation by law and four of which permitted local option.

School desegregation through integration thus became the first racial problem to be pressed in the movement. Almost exactly a year later, the Supreme Court ordered that the process of desegregation must proceed "with all deliberate speed." Reaction in the South varied from outright opposition to cautious delay and "tokenism" (limited obedience). The first violence and riots were not long in coming.

At the opening of schools in September 1956 the town of Clinton, Tennessee, seethed with mob hatred and violent resistance encouraged by out-of-state racist agitators, until quieted by state highway patrolmen and the National Guard.

The first serious major riot occurred when the law was applied to the Central High School of Little Rock, Arkan-

sas, in September 1957. Governor Orval Faubus posted
National Guardsmen at the entrance of the all-white
school to prevent nine pupils from entering. When the
guardsmen were removed by federal injunction the children again attempted to enter, but a mob of belligerent
and shrieking demonstrators forced them to leave. Federal
troops, a thousand paratroopers, were finally called out
to protect the Negroes and quiet the mobs.

Attempts of Negroes to enroll in institutions of higher
education varied from a few registrations accompanied
by protests, but without incidents or violence, to the full-
scale riot that broke out on September 30-October 1, 1962,
when James Meredith, escorted by several hundred United
States marshals, attempted to take up residence on the
campus of the University of Mississippi at Oxford and
enroll as its first Negro student. Two men were killed and
scores injured during a fifteen-hour battle between students and federal troops. This riot formed a perfect
modern example of crowd action under stress.

At Oxford all the factors leading to violent mob behavior were present—time for a build-up of tension, with
advance notice that the registration attempt would be
resisted, a gradual increase in the size of the assembled
crowd, rumors and counterrumors, absence of restraint by
local police and their failure to take immediate action
to disperse the crowd or control the agitators and ha-
ranguers, and, finally, the participation of non-students
who had nothing whatever to do with the university or
the problem.

The initial resistance of the highest state officials until
served with court orders, and the open opposition of the

riotous students, overcome only by the use of tanks and tear gas, shocked the country. The battle for equality of educational opportunity on all school levels is still being fought in both the South and the North, but for the most part through court cases and federal action.

Negroes have been personally involved in demanding other of their constitutional rights—integration of public accommodations, desegregation in housing, non-discriminatory employment opportunities, and, finally, in the Southern states, registration as voters according to the guarantees in the Civil Rights Act of 1957 and the Voting Rights Act of 1965.

To emphasize their determination to gain these rights, a method of protest called "nonviolent direct action," begun in December 1955 at Montgomery, Alabama, has been extensively used. The method is comparable to labor's substitution of mediation, conciliation, and legal picketing for the frequent violence of the past in settling disputes and satisfying worker demands.

This technique of nonviolence has been patterned after the mass passive resistance of Mahatma Gandhi, leader of the people of India in their struggle for independence from Great Britain during the 1930s and 1940s. While imprisoned in Cape Colony, South Africa, for leading nonviolent protests against the non-admittance of Indians into the state of Transvaal as immigrants in 1908, Gandhi read a lecture by Henry David Thoreau titled "The Rights and Duties of the Individual in Relation to Government," printed in 1849 under the changed title "Civil Disobedience."

While living at Walden in 1846, Thoreau had been

arrested and jailed for refusing to pay his taxes in protest against the Mexican War. The author maintained that an individual, to protect his own integrity, was justified in not obeying laws of which he did not morally approve. He might not be successful, but his resistance could eventually change the laws; at least the individual's non-cooperation could serve to call attention to the flaws. Although Thoreau's theory of non-cooperation was an individual one, Gandhi's was collective, as a means of mass protest. Gandhi coined the word *satyagraha,* literally translated as "truth force" but meaning struggle without violence.

The nonviolent form of Negro protest was first used in Montgomery, Alabama, during 1955-56, in a successful boycott of the local segregated bus system. Under the leadership of the Rev. Martin Luther King, Jr., minister of the Dexter Avenue Baptist Church in Montgomery at the time, the technique was applied locally, then throughout both the South and the North as a means of demanding the rights of Negroes as citizens and of appealing to the consciences of right-minded citizens everywhere.

The deeply religious overtones of the nonviolent doctrine are described by Dr. King in his book, *Why We Can't Wait:* "It was not a doctrine that made their [the sponsoring Negro ministers] followers yearn for revenge but one that called upon them to champion social change. It was not a doctrine that asked an eye for an eye but one that summoned men to seek to open the eyes of blind prejudice. The Negro turned his back on force not only because he knew he could not win his freedom through physical force but also because he believed that through physical force he could lose his soul."

The nonviolent protest is aimed basically at dramatizing the plight of the Negro, gaining recognition of his legally guaranteed rights, and forcing legal action to bring them to reality. The specific techniques used are many—public demonstrations of all sorts, freedom rides, freedom and prayer marches (with placard carrying and singing), sit-ins (borrowed from the early days of labor strikes), sit-downs, kneel-ins (on the steps of segregated churches), lie-downs, and boycotts.

Interpreting Thoreau's and Gandhi's beliefs, Dr. King maintains that "there are two types of laws, just and unjust. One has not only a legal but a moral responsibility to obey just laws. Conversely, one has a moral responsibility to disobey unjust laws." He applies this to the Negro problem: "Any law that uplifts human personality is just; any law that degrades human personality is unjust. All segregation statutes and ordinances are unjust because segregation distorts the soul and damages the personality."

Of the practice of civil disobedience Dr. King writes: "One who breaks an unjust law must do so openly, lovingly, and with a willingness to accept the penalty. I submit that an individual who breaks a law that conscience tells him is unjust and who willingly accepts the penalty of imprisonment in order to arouse the conscience of the community over its injustice, is in reality expressing the highest respect for law."

Thousands of demonstrators, both Negro and white, have been arrested while practicing civil disobedience in the nonviolent direct action movement. Local law enforcement agencies have been forced to determine when, under their local ordinances and court rulings, a peaceful demonstration becomes an unlawful assemblage, "a public nuisance," a disturbance of the peace, or "a breach of the peace," i.e., disorderly conduct. A sit-down in a store or at a lunch counter may be considered as trespassing. Some communities require parade permits for demonstrations, others forbid them completely. When groups defy such local rules and prohibitions under the doctrine of civil disobedience, with its acceptance of the arrest penalty, anti-Negro violence frequently occurs.

No single aspect of the civil rights movement has proved to be so controversial. Agents of law enforcement are almost unanimous in their condemnation and opposition, pointing out the fact that if civil disobedience is valid for a small violation it might apply equally to a more serious one. The result, they maintain, would eventually be a complete disregard for the orderly process of law.

In August 1965 United States District Judge Frank M. Johnson, Jr., ruling in the cases of 167 demonstrators arrested in Montgomery, Alabama, stated: "The philosophy that a person may determine for himself what laws and court decisions are morally right or wrong and either obey or refuse to obey them according to his own determination is a philosophy that is foreign to our 'rule of law' theory of government." Arrest and prosecution in such cases, Judge Johnson maintained, are absolutely necessary if the existing laws are to be upheld.

With notable and much-publicized exceptions, many

clergymen have expressed support of the doctrine and practice of civil disobedience on moral grounds. A "position" paper of the House of Bishops of the 61st General Convention of the Protestant Episcopal Church in 1964 may be cited as typical of the stand taken by many religious leaders collectively or as individuals.

"Under all normal circumstances," the statement read, "Christians obey the civil law, seeing in it the will of God. Yet it must be recognized that laws exist which deny these external and immutable laws. In such case the Church and its members . . . reserve the right to obey God rather than man."

The crux of the paper follows:

"Thus, the Church recognizes the rights of any persons to urge the repeal of unjust laws by all lawful means, including participation in *peaceful* demonstrations. If and when the means of legal recourse have been exhausted or are demonstrably inadequate, the Church recognizes the right of all persons for reasons of informed conscience to disobey such laws, so long as such persons:

a) accept the just penalty for their action;
b) carry out their protest in a non-violent manner;
c) exercise severe restraint in using this privilege of conscience, because of the danger of lawlessness attendant thereto."

The danger of violence and even riot is ever present in nonviolent protests. This technique, continuously, methodically, and doggedly used, has often enraged the agencies of local and state law enforcement. The result has been a stiffening of white resistance to Negro pressures for civil rights which on more than one occasion has erupted into anti-Negro race riots and violence. These clashes have in most cases been initiated by white police against nonviolent Negro demonstrators, resulting in charges of police brutality.

Only a few of the principal incidents of violence by both whites and Negroes will be cited here, as examples of the movement's scope and its opposition.

Early demonstrations in the South were sit-ins aimed toward the desegregation of public facilities such as stores, lunch counters and restaurants, libraries, theaters, swimming pools, and lavatories and rest rooms. Countless arrests and even incidents of beatings were reported.

The movement for segregation in transportation, including the use of terminal facilities, was initiated by the freedom rides from Washington, D.C., into the Deep South. Both whites and Negroes participated.

The first riot against nonviolent protesters occurred in May 1961 when a biracial group of student freedom riders arrived in Montgomery, Alabama, to protest bus-terminal segregation. A crowd of more than a thousand awaited them; the disorder was put down only when tear gas was used and almost four hundred United States marshals had been dispatched to Montgomery by the Department of Justice. The immediate result was that the Interstate Commerce Commission outlawed segregation in all trains and buses and in terminals (waiting rooms and lunch counters). Other less spectacular incidents of violence followed.

In subsequent months and years police excesses have

become common. The use of police dogs, night sticks (clubs), whips, fire hoses, tear gas, and electric cattle prods has affirmed the existence of a hard core of resistance and intense opposition among Southerners, yet at the same time has strengthened the determination and resolution of the nonviolent protesters. Incidents in Birmingham and Selma, Alabama, and Princess Anne, Maryland, particularly, and widespread police and white brutality have received world-wide attention.

White civilians have on many occasions staged their own riotous protests against Negro demonstrators. For example, in St. Augustine, Florida, in June 1964, a white mob of eight hundred attacked a freedom march. Thirty Negroes and three whites were hospitalized, and the mob forced the police to free four whites who had been arrested.

Nor have all Negroes heeded Martin Luther King's example and practice of nonviolence. Following tragic incidents or setbacks, Negroes themselves rioted in protest. One of the worst of these riots took place in Birmingham on May 7, 1963, following the mass arrest and imprisonment of twenty-five hundred demonstrators, including Dr. King. The use of high-pressure fire hoses and police dogs to halt the protest demonstration triggered the disorder. About three thousand adult Negroes, without any obvious leadership or plan, ran wild through the business district, smashing shop windows and stealing their contents. They resisted the police by throwing rocks and bricks in pitched battles until finally forced back into the segregated colored district by fire hoses and armored police cars. Only when state troopers were summoned was order restored, and twelve hundred law officers were finally on guard to maintain order in the tense city.

White resistance has found expression in individual anarchic and criminal acts of all types, including murder, shooting, arson, and bombing. Two particular incidents— the assassination of Medgar Evers, NAACP secretary for the state of Mississippi, in Jackson on June 13, 1963, and the bombing of a Birmingham Baptist church on a Sunday morning in September 1963, in which four Negro children were killed—shocked the country so profoundly that public outrage and pressure literally demanded the passage of the Civil Rights Act of 1964.

The dramatic March on Washington for Jobs and Freedom on August 28, 1963, in which 250,000 Negroes and whites jointly participated, was the first national demonstration to alert millions of their fellow citizens that the civil rights movement was an activity of *all* Negroes, and that they would continue to press to become first-class citizens. "Jobs and freedom" were the goals that expressed the Negroes' discontent in the North and the South.

Negroes would no longer accept their rights piecemeal. As Dr. King has pointed out, the civil rights movement is not a revolt, it is a revolution in every sense of the word. He made this distinction in the statement: "A social movement that only moves people is merely a revolt. A movement that changes both people and institutions is a revolution."

Bayard Rustin, one of the organizers of the march, has pointed out that "the Freedom Movement, though it eschews violence and is committed to the social processes of democracy, is inherently revolutionary."

Anthony Lewis, New York *Times* Washington correspondent covering the Supreme Court and the Justice Department, maintains that the 1954 Supreme Court decision against segregation started this "social revolution."

The "Second American Revolution" by our country's largest minority group has as its war cry "Freedom— Now!" and its rallying song is "We Shall Overcome."

This social upheaval calls for a complete re-examination of everything American democracy stands for. The potentially explosive situations throughout the Deep South and in the slums of the largest Northern cities will continue to erupt into violence and riots until the Negro goal of complete freedom is achieved.

16

Contemporary Tensions and Unrest

A FUTURE commentator on the American scene may well characterize the late 1950s and the 1960s as an era of protest and violence. Scanning the headlines of the period, he will be certain of reading the oft-repeated words "protest," "demonstration," "vandalism," "attack," and even "riot." Accounts of crime will include murder, rape, shooting, assault, robbery, burglary, larceny, and auto theft. Reports of violence, in fact, have become so commonplace as to be accepted without question as a part of the fabric of contemporary life.

Certainly the right of peaceful protest is a part of our American heritage of freedom. In hailing the passage of the Voting Rights Bill of 1965, President Lyndon Johnson made these observations on rights: "So, free speech, free press, free religion, the right of free assembly, yes, the right of petition, the right to buy ads and to have teach-ins, and sit-ins, and parades and marches and demonstrations—well, they're still radical ideas. And so are secret ballots, and so are free elections, and so is the principle of

158

equal dignity, and so is the principle of equal rights for all the sons and daughters of man. But all of these things are what America stands for, and all of these things are what you and all other Americans need to stand up for today."

More and more often, however, protest is taking the form of lawlessness in insane explosions of violence and riot.

The most shocking and terrifying examples of such contemporary lawlessness have been the Negro riots in Northern cities during two recent summers—seven in 1964 and one in 1965. Unlike the riots of the civil rights movement, these were, in the words of Theodore H. White in *The Making of the President—1964*, "riots of black men and adolescents against the conditions of life they have found within the ghettos of the big city." Mr. White continues: "They were anarchy, a revolt led by wild youth against authority, against discipline, against the orderly government of a society that had taken too long to pay them heed." Furthermore, they were insurrections under the Webster's Dictionary definition of the word: "a rising up against civil or political authority."

The Federal Bureau of Investigation report on the 1964 riots characterized them as "senseless attacks upon all constituted authority without purpose or object." The report continued: "They were not a direct outgrowth of conventional civil rights protests"; indeed, most responsible leaders have specifically deplored the violence and expressed fears that such riots can inflict untold harm upon the nonviolent movement. The report emphasized that the "mob violence was dominated by the acts of youths ranging in age to the middle twenties." The latter are the underprivileged youths who live imprisoned in urban ghettos, most of them from broken homes and with a hopeless future.

A common feature of all these riots is that they were triggered in nearly every instance by an encounter, or a rumored encounter, between a white policeman (or policemen) and a Negro (or Negroes) in which the former was believed to have used undue force.

This animosity toward the police, usually charged to "police brutality," apparently springs from the honest conviction of many Negroes that they do not and will not receive the same treatment as white citizens in an encounter with the law and that, if arrested, they are likely to be handled roughly by the police.

The 1964 and 1965 summer riots each began with a police incident and followed a more or less common pattern—first, the detention or arrest of a Negro for a traffic violation or fighting, or the spreading rumor of an incident of "police brutality." Typically, a crowd gathers and mills about, muttering threats and joining in the arguments. This crowd increases in size until the individuals become members of a mob. The more vocal leaders begin to stir the emotions and police hatred of all within earshot. Missiles, rocks, bottles, and bricks are thrown at the police. Rumors circulate freely and are passed without being checked for accuracy and with further elaboration. Finally the violence spreads to white-owned stores and businesses; systematic destruction and looting then begins. There may also be burning, shooting, and individual encounters with the police, and the mob may eventually break up into roving gangs.

Statistics are useful only in recording the tangibles of these riots. The figures below are taken from the report of the Governor's Commission on the Los Angeles Riots of 1965. They indicate the human toll dead, injured, and arrested, and show the damage:

City	Date	Killed	Injured	Arrests	Stores Damaged
New York City (Harlem and Brooklyn)	July 18–23, 1964	1	144	519	541
Rochester, N.Y.	July 24–25	4	350	976	204
Jersey City, N.J.	August 2–4	0	46	52	71
Paterson, N.J.	August 11–13	0	8	65	20
Elizabeth, N.J.	August 11–13	0	6	18	17
Chicago, Ill. (Dixmoor)	August 16–17	0	57	80	2
Philadelphia, Pa.	August 28–30	0	341	774	225
	1965				
Los Angeles, Calif. (Watts)	August 11–17	34	1032	3952	600

Appalling as these figures are, they do not show the individual situations, the scope of the disorder, the countless tragic incidents, or most of all the causes behind the disturbances and the relation of the riots to the Negro revolution. The short accounts that follow can serve only to indicate the basic facts.

The racial violence that erupted in the Harlem section of New York City on July 18, 1964, was attributed to tensions aroused by the slaying of a fifteen-year-old Negro schoolboy two days before by a white police officer who had reportedly been attacked with a knife. The riot continued for four days despite stern police anti-riot action, including the firing of thousands of warning shots into the air. Negro mobs, large and small, broke windows, looted

stores, hurled debris at the police, and assaulted a few
white people in the area. The next day the riot fever broke
out in the predominantly Negro Bedford-Stuyvesant section of Brooklyn, with crowds of roving, rampaging Negroes looting stores in a wide area.

On July 24 racial unrest flared up in Rochester, New
York. The riot started with a rumor that two policemen
had clubbed and kicked two Negroes fighting at a street
dance, when in fact they had only attempted to stop the
altercation. For two days angry mobs smashed and looted
white-owned stores, the property damage reaching several
million dollars. The violence ended only after New York
National Guard units and state troopers were sent to aid
local police in restoring order.

The epidemic spread to New Jersey, where Negroes in
Jersey City attacked police and looted stores on August
2-4 after a rumor of police brutality against an arrested
Negro. A week later Paterson seethed with unrest and
clashes, the flare-up resulting when Negro youths leaving
a city-sponsored dance threw rocks at police cars on the
night of August 11, the violence spreading to Elizabeth.

Soon after, the integrated Chicago suburb of Dixmoor
was the setting of a full-scale riot which broke out after a
rumor spread that a white liquor store owner had attacked
a Negro woman whom he accused of shoplifting a bottle
of gin. The clash began when police attempted to arrest
her. Almost a thousand Negroes fought with 225 state
troopers and police for two days. The liquor store was
looted and set afire, and fifty automobiles were damaged.

The final summer riot of 1964, just before Labor Day,
was in North Philadelphia, Pennsylvania, in which 200,000

Negroes lived. Triggered by a false rumor that a policeman had killed a Negro woman who refused to leave a stalled car that blocked an intersection, gangs roamed over a four-square-mile area, systematically damaging and looting stores, with losses estimated at $2,500,000.

Property damage and fire insurance companies were reported to have taken an estimated $257,750,000 underwriting loss from the 1964 riots. These riots, plus the Los Angeles 1965 riot, have caused the insurance industry to revise coverage policies; many contracts for urban slum areas have been canceled or rates substantially increased.

The 1964 riots alerted government officials and agencies, both federal and local, to the plight of Negroes in the slum areas of the Northern cities. Some progress was made during the year by the introduction of a large number of varied anti-poverty programs: job training, special schools for dropouts, and the like.

But just as the programs were emerging from the governmental red tape, the Watts section of Los Angeles became the setting in August 1965 for a widespread and destructive riot which made those of the previous summer seem minor in comparison.

Watts is a congested area that holds some 80,000 people, ninety-nine per cent Negro, in the southeastern part of Los Angeles. The Watts district is unlike the Negro slum areas of the Eastern cities, for the wide streets are lined with palm trees, spacious lawns, and small bungalow houses, many of which, however, are dilapidated and overcrowded.

But underneath the pleasant exterior the Watts citizens exhibit all the characteristics of the underprivileged minorities in large Northern cities. Two thirds have less than a high school education, the rate of school dropout being exceptionally high. One eighth are illiterate. Nearly thirty per cent of the children are from fatherless homes; a study of four hundred arrested juvenile rioters gave the figure as almost seventy-five per cent.

Indeed, this deterioration of the Negro family unit, with broken, mother-dominated homes and a high rate of illegitimacy, has been continuously pointed out, most notably in a United States Department of Labor study, *The Negro Family: The Case for National Action*, popularly known as the Moynihan Report. Its author, Daniel P. Moynihan, wrote it while serving as Assistant Secretary of Labor. These children, according to Theodore White, grow up to be teenage savages, "an element that no one knows how to handle. Denied love or dignity or patrimony or tradition or any culture but television, they rock around on the deck of an unstable society, their hopes zero, their mothers despised, their hearth the gutter."

Over a three-month period prior to the Watts insurrection, police reported ninety-six major crimes, including murders, rapes, and assaults in the area. The unemployment rate is two to three times the national urban average.

Watts urgently needed assistance of all types—urban renewal, anti-poverty programs, and job training. But little had been done when, on Wednesday evening, August 11, 1965, the riot began in an anti-police incident similar in pattern to the 1964 uprisings in the Northeastern cities.

A state motorcycle trooper stopped a Negro youth after a six-block chase and gave him a standard Highway Patrol sobriety test, which he failed. The officer told him he was under arrest. The boy's mother came from their home nearby and scolded her son for being intoxicated. A crowd of onlookers watched as the boy started to resist arrest and struggled with the patrolman, who radioed for help and drew his shotgun. When help arrived the prisoner was subdued and taken to the police station. His mother and brother, who had attacked the officers, were arrested and charged with disorderly conduct.

The group of spectators, which had grown from twenty-five to three hundred, resented the use of force, and as their number increased to a final thousand, rumor took over. The story of police brutality was that the prisoner had been beaten up and dragged away. The word spread and suddenly, in the darkness, rocks began to be thrown, aimed at passing cars and stores.

Unlucky white motorists were bombarded with empty bottles, slabs of concrete, rocks, bricks, nuts, bolts, boards, and chunks of asphalt pavement. The white police who arrived to maintain order only increased the fury of the Negroes. All through the night gangs roamed the area, overturning and burning vehicles, including two fire trucks.

In spite of the presence of a substantial police force during the next day, a mob estimated at seven thousand swarmed through the streets on Thursday night, armed with Molotov cocktails. (These are glass bottles filled with gasoline and corked. Around the neck of each bottle a piece of gasoline-soaked rag is tied. The rag is set afire and the bottle thrown.) Large numbers were hurled on any interesting target. A lumberyard, a clinic, a chain store, a restaurant, a liquor store went up in flames. Most of these businesses were owned by absentee whites. "Whitey" was the common enemy and the object of the mob's wrath; scores of white drivers were dragged from their cars and beaten, and the cars set afire.

All through Friday the wanton destruction continued uncontrolled until National Guardsmen arrived late at night. Looters were active everywhere, clearing shelves of stores before setting the premises afire. Only when sniping gunfire was returned and a strict curfew imposed on the area for three days did the insurrection cease. By its end the disorder had spread until ultimately an area covering forty-six and a half square miles had to be controlled with the aid of military authority.

An analysis of the statistics in the previous table indicates the magnitude of the toll. Of the injured, 90 were police officers, 136 firemen, 10 National Guardsmen, 23 government agency officials, and 773 civilians. Of the 600 buildings damaged by burning and looting, more than a third were totally destroyed by fire. Between two and three thousand fire alarms were recorded during the riot. More than seventy per cent of the arrests (3,400 adults, 552 juveniles) were for burglary and theft. Unsubstantiated estimates of the property damage were as high as $100,000,000, $40,000,000 for fire alone.

The responsible Negro leaders of the civil rights movement were the first to deplore the lawlessness, which did immeasurable damage to the essentially nonviolent cause. President Johnson condemned the uprising, saying, "A rioter with a Molotov cocktail in his hands is not fighting for civil rights any more than a Klansman with a sheet on his back and a mask on his face. They are both more or

less what the law declares them: lawbreakers, destroyers
of Constitutional rights and liberties, and ultimately destroyers of a free America."

Sociologists, psychologists, and public officials began to
seek the causes of the insurrection. A Governor's Commission on the Los Angeles Riots, appointed by California
Governor Edmund G. Brown and headed by John A.
McCone, conducted a hundred-day inquiry and issued its
report under the title *Violence in the City—An End or
a Beginning?* The riot was characterized as "not a race riot
in the usual sense, but an explosion—a formless, quite
senseless, all but hopeless violent protest."

The causes cited were much the same as those leading
to the riots of the 1964 summer—not enough jobs and a
lack of training for Negroes; lack of schooling designed
to meet the special needs of the Negro child, whose en-
vironment from infancy onward places him under a serious
handicap; and a resentment, even hatred, of the police as
symbols of authority. Specific recommendations were
made in the areas of employment, education, welfare and
health, and local law enforcement.

All concerned with the plight of the Negro citizen as
the number one social problem in our country freely express the opinion that more riots may occur. But threats
of racial violence will disappear as legal discrimination is
removed, barriers to voting are eliminated, and when
schooling and jobs are available to all. These changes will
take time. The Negro revolution is certain to continue.

An ever present danger in all demonstrations is that
opposition groups may attempt to interfere and break up

the peaceful protest. The fact that the subject or cause is worthy of sincere and serious protest means that it is controversial. Its opponents may undertake their own method of protest—a counterdemonstration. The preliminary jeers and heckling may result in a scuffle which, if not immediately stopped by police, can very easily develop into serious violence and possibly into a full-scale riot.

The police of most cities now receive instruction and training in crowd as well as riot control, and arrests during protest demonstrations are usually for disturbing the peace and disorderly conduct.

A large percentage of the participants in present-day demonstrations are college students. The reason for this is generally attributed to the adolescent's intense devotion to causes, his keen sense of right and wrong, and his need for self-expression.

The current protest demonstrations of university and college students cover a wide range of causes and grievances. They are carrying over into the campus the tactics of civil disobedience developed in the Southern nonviolent civil rights movement.

The sit-in at the University of California (at Berkeley) in December 1964 had as its object the attainment of freedom to engage in political activity on the campus grounds. In addition to taking over Sproul Hall, an administrative building, for a sixteen-hour sit-in, some of the students surrounded and detained for thirty-six hours a police car and its occupants that had come to the campus to take a leader of the demonstrators to jail. More than eight hundred students in the all-night sit-in were arrested for trespassing.

Other protest demonstrations of students at Berkeley and other universities have served to express their dissatisfaction with education in a large university, and their desire for free political expression and speech, and their need to revolt against the conventional ideas of their parents.

In the many analyses of these protests, writers have cited the need for adolescents to express themselves freely and to accept no longer the ideas of their elders and teachers. This form of "rebellion," a psychologist has asserted, is a part of youth's "growing pains in a turbulent and insecure society where the atom bomb is a constant threat."

Many teenagers of high school age have also adopted the prevailing spirit of revolt and protest. Most of the nation's twenty-four million teens are not particularly interested in "causes"—their problems are much more personal. But the noisy, vocal, and often lawless minority of extremists unfortunately occupies the center of the stage and gains more attention nationally.

The astonishing growth of teenage lawlessness is both shocking and frightening. Commenting on the increase in both crime and arrests, F.B.I. Director J. Edgar Hoover cited the many summer riots and gang "rumbles," and the senseless vandalism that is becoming increasingly prevalent.

Riots involving teenagers have come to be annual traditions of Labor Day weekend, the last before the schools open. Indeed, certain resorts have learned from repeated experience to anticipate yearly riots. Two of the most destructive in 1964 were investigated by the F.B.I., together with the seven major Negro riots. Both occurred on the first weekend of September.

At Seaside, Oregon, for the third year, teenagers tried to storm into the main street of the town from the beach area on which they had been restricted by roadblocks. On Saturday night about eight hundred youths (compared with two thousand the previous year) cursed and pelted the state police and National Guardsmen on alert duty with rocks and sand-filled beer cans when their way was effectively barred. The next night a hundred and fifty more repeated the attack. A total of a hundred youths were arrested.

Across the continent at Hampton Beach, New Hampshire, for the fourth consecutive year, seven thousand teenagers celebrated their vacations' end by surging through the streets from the beach, throwing bottles and trash everywhere. Several fires were set and hundreds of windows shattered. They attacked police who had ordered them to disperse, and firemen used high-pressure hoses to break up the riot. When the rioters continued racing through the streets, Governor John King called out National Guard units, who blocked the streets, their bayonets ready for use, while rocks, clubs, and beer cans rained upon them from darkness until dawn. At its height ten thousand youths were involved, and Maine state troopers were also summoned. Arrests numbered a hundred and fifty.

The most publicized incident of vandalism on this 1964 Labor Day weekend took place at Southampton, Long Island, where young guests at a "debut" party made a shambles of a shore-front mansion rented for them. Since these teenagers were from wealthy families their destructiveness was the more difficult to explain.

In his report on youthful crime Mr. Hoover stated: "Even if 'society' has failed our youth, this does not condone rebellious conduct against authority, law and order, or any regulatory measures which restrict their whims, wishes, desires, and activities."

Participants in today's riots, if arrested, may be punished according to penalties prescribed in either federal, state, or local laws. Rioters or demonstrators may be arrested on a variety of charges; the most common are disturbing the peace and disorderly conduct. All individuals in a group can be charged with unlawful assembly, particularly when the police have ordered them to disperse. Apprehended looters are held on larceny charges of various degrees.

Each member of what the law terms a "riotous assembly" is himself guilty of riot and may be punished accordingly. Under the law, joining a group at any time during a disturbance makes an individual subject to arrest for riot; there is no such thing as an "innocent bystander" caught in mob action. In common law rioting is a misdemeanor punishable by fine or imprisonment. The penalties are more severe when rioters are armed. Sometimes, as in the case of William Epton, one of the acknowledged leaders of the 1964 Harlem summer riot, the charge was conspiracy and criminal anarchy; he received a one-year sentence on the latter charge.

Modern riots and mob violence inflict two kinds of damage, human and property. The laws of some states provide compensation for personal injuries sustained dur-

ing or as a result of riot, to be paid by the municipality in
which the riot took place. The lack of witnesses, however,
makes personal injury cases difficult to prove under the
law of evidence.

Uninsured victims of looting, property damage, and fire
may file damage suits charging negligence and inadequate protection by city, county, and state officials. A principle of common law is that government has an absolute
responsibility to stop riots. No matter how hard police
try to prevent them, such losses are regarded as evidence
that the three types of local government failed to use
enough force to prevent disorder.

Almost without exception insurance companies pay for
property damages and such losses from fire and robbery
under what is termed the standard "riot and commotion"
coverage. Most policies also include a standard clause ex-
cluding coverage for fire, rioting, or looting during "war
and insurrection." However, most of the many companies
which had underwritten policies in the Watts area have
paid claims under the "riot" clause, thus choosing not to
term the Los Angeles riot an "insurrection."

The chronology and pattern of the uprisings in this book
indicate that they were a part of the growing pains of
our development as a democracy. Protests and riots may
call attention to conditions needing correction and may
lead to remedial actions or measures such as full-scale investigations and legislation.

But the dangers and futility of rioting are repeatedly
demonstrated with statistics of casualties and physical
damage and accounts of the scars inflicted on human re-

lationships, the encouragement of mutual distrust, and the frequent increase rather than decrease of tensions afterward. More often than not, violence stiffens the determination of the opposition and makes the path of the rioters more difficult.

It should be noted that substitutes for violence are being used today in many areas. Labor strikes, work stoppages, lockouts, and sit-downs, for example, are usually settled by the use of established channels for the airing of grievances and the employment of mediation, arbitration, and collective bargaining. The strike of New York City transit workers in January 1966, though paralyzing our country's largest metropolis, was entirely free of violence. The methods of protest in the civil rights movement have in many cases avoided violence.

Protesters against injustices are more and more depending upon the law for adjustments and solutions, even though to the impatient the legal process may seem deliberate and painfully slow. Compliance of Southern public school systems with the federal law on school desegregation, for example, is being sought in the courts.

The extremists and restless elements in our population have always fomented and will continue to foment disorders. Nonetheless, as Plutarch said in his life of Sertorius, "Perseverance is more prevailing than violence, and many things which cannot be overcome when they are together yield themselves up when taken little by little."

SOURCES
AND
READINGS

Chapter 1—The Anatomy of Riot

CROWD AND GROUP BEHAVIOR

All volumes of social psychology include discussions of group behavior. Below are a few recommended titles.

Le Bon, Gustave. *The Crowd: A Study of the Popular Mind.* N.Y., Viking Press, 1960. Paperback ed., Compass Books C66.
Martin, Everett Dean. *The Behavior of Crowds.* N.Y., Harper, 1920.
Ogburn, William F., and Nimkoff, M. F. *Sociology.* 3d ed. Boston, Houghton Mifflin, 1958. pp. 199-225.
Rudé, George F. E. *The Crowd in the French Revolution.* N.Y., Oxford University Press, 1950.
Young, Kimball. *Social Psychology.* 3d ed. N.Y., Appleton-Century-Crofts, 1956. pp. 286-309.

MOB AND RIOT CONTROL

Applegate, Rex. *Crowd and Riot Control.* 6th ed. Harrisburg, Stackpole, 1964. pp. 23-33.
Curry, J. E., and King, G. D. *Race Tensions and the Police.* Springfield, Ill., C. C. Thomas, 1962. pp. 61-73.
Towler, Juby E. *Police Role in Racial Conflicts.* Springfield, Ill., C. C. Thomas, 1964.

ANTI-AMERICAN MOBS

Methvin, Eugene H. "How the Reds Make a Riot." *Reader's Digest,* Vol. 86 (January 1965), pp. 63-69.
"Record of Outrages and the Protocol of Protection." *Life,* Vol. 58 (March 19, 1965), p. 38B.

Chapter 2—Stamp Act Riots

Every book on American Colonial history deals with the resistance to the Stamp Act, often briefly. Below are some of the longer discussions.

Gipson, Lawrence H. *The Coming of the Revolution, 1763-1775.* N.Y., Harper & Bros., 1954. pp. 85-100.

Headley, Joel T. *The Great Riots of New York, 1712 to 1873.* N.Y., Treat, 1873. pp. 46-55.

Jennings, John. *Boston: Cradle of Liberty.* Garden City, N.Y., Doubleday, 1947. pp. 155-160.

Labaree, Benjamin W. *The Road to Independence, 1763-1776.* N.Y., Macmillan, 1963. pp. 15-28.

Longley, R. S. "Mob Activities in Revolutionary Massachusetts." *New England Quarterly,* Vol. 6 (1933), pp. 98-130.

Miller, John C. *Origins of the American Revolution.* Boston, Little, Brown, 1943. pp. 115-126, 129-132, 142-143.

Morgan, Edmund S., and Helen M. *The Stamp Act Crisis.* Chapel Hill, University of North Carolina Press, 1953. pp. 123-132, 144-158.

Schlesinger, Arthur M. "Political Mobs and the American Revolution, 1765-1776." *American Philosophical Society Proceedings,* Vol. 99 (August 1955), pp. 244-250.

Chapter 3—Doctors' Riot

Booth, Mary L. *History of the City of New York.* N.Y., Dutton, 1880. pp. 583-586.

Edwards, L. F. "Resurrection (Body Snatching) Riots During the Heroic Age of Anatomy in America." *Bulletin of the History of Medicine,* Vol. 25 (March-April 1951), pp. 174-184.

Headley, Joel T. *The Great Riots of New York, 1712 to 1873.* N.Y., Treat, 1873. pp. 56-65.

Heaton, C. E. "Body Snatching in New York City." *New York State Journal of Medicine,* Vol. 43 (October 1, 1943), pp. 1861-1865.

Ladenheim, J. C. "Doctors' Mob of 1788; Importance in Practice of Dissection in U.S." *Journal of the History of Medicine and Allied Sciences,* Vol. 5 (Winter 1950), pp. 23-43.

Stone, William H. *History of New York City.* N.Y., Virtue & Yorston, 1872. pp. 231-236.

Victor, Ralph G. "An Indictment for Grave Robbing at the Time of the Doctors' Riot." *Annals of Medical History,* 3d Series, Vol. 2 (1940), pp. 366-367.

Walsh, James J. *History of Medicine in New York.* N.Y., National Americana Society, 1919. Vol. 2, pp. 378-392.

Chapter 4—Anti-Catholic Riots

"The Anti-Catholic Riots of 1844 in Philadelphia," an eyewitness account. *American Catholic Historical Researches,* Vol. 13 (April 1896), pp. 50-64.
Billington, Ray A. *The Protestant Crusade, 1800-1860.* N.Y., Macmillan, 1938. pp. 220-237.
Henry, Sister M. St. "Nativism in Pennsylvania." *American Catholic Historical Society of Philadelphia. Record,* Vol. 47 (March 1936), pp. 5-47, esp. pp. 20-33.
Kirlin, Joseph L. J. *Catholicity in Philadelphia.* Philadelphia, McVey, 1909. pp. 304-337.
McMaster, John B. *History of the People of the United States.* N.Y., Appleton, 1910. Vol. 7, pp. 373-385.
Myers, Gustavus. *History of Bigotry in the United States.* N.Y., Capricorn Books, 1960 (Originally published by Random House, 1943). Chapter XII, Nativism, pp. 110-125.
Repplier, Agnes. *Philadelphia: The Place and the People.* N.Y., Macmillan, 1898. pp. 342-355.
Scharf, John T., and Westcott, Thompson. *History of Philadelphia.* Philadelphia, Everts & Co., 1884. Vol. 1, pp. 663-672.
Shea, John G. *A History of the Catholic Church in the United States.* N.Y., Shea, 1886. Vol. 4, pp. 46-55.

Chapter 5—Astor Place Riot

Bales, William A. *Tiger in the Streets.* N.Y., Dodd Mead, 1962. pp. 38-43.
"Charge to Grand Jury by Judge Daly in the case of Astor Place Riot." *Western Law Journal,* Vol. 7 (November 1849), pp. 68-75.
Headley, Joel T. *The Great Riots of New York, 1712 to 1873.* N.Y., Treat, 1873. pp. 111-128.
Minnigerode, Meade. *The Fabulous Forties.* N.Y., G. P. Putnam's Sons, 1924. pp. 187-209.
Monaghan, Jay. *The Great Rascal: Life and Adventures of Ned Buntline.* Boston, Little, Brown, 1952. pp. 170-180.
Moody, Richard. *The Astor Place Riot.* Bloomington, Indiana University Press, 1958.
Wilson, James G. *Memorial History of New York City.* N.Y., New York History Co., 1892-1893. Vol. 3, pp. 430-435.

Chapter 6—Draft Riots

Asbury, Herbert. *The Gangs of New York*. N.Y., Knopf, 1927. pp. 118-171.
Bales, William A. *Tiger in the Streets*. N.Y., Dodd Mead, 1962. pp. 125-148.
Booth, Mary L. *History of the City of New York*. N.Y., Dutton, 1880. pp. 818-833.
Headley, Joel T. *The Great Riots of New York, 1712 to 1873*. N.Y., Treat, 1873. pp. 136-288.
Lader, Lawrence. "New York's Bloodiest Week." *American Heritage*, Vol. 10 (June 1959), pp. 44-49, 95-98.
McMaster, John B. *A History of the People of the United States During Lincoln's Administration*. N.Y., Appleton, 1927. pp. 407-415.
Sandburg, Carl. *Abraham Lincoln: The War Years*. N.Y., Harcourt, 1926. Vol. 2, pp. 360-369, 370-377.
Stone, William L. *History of New York City*. N.Y., Virtue & Yorston, 1872. pp. 539-562.
Werstein, Irving. *July, 1863*. N.Y., Messner, 1957. Paperback, Ace Book, D-325.

Chapter 7—Anti-Chinese Riot

Bell, Horace. *On the Old West Coast*. N.Y., Morrow, 1930. pp. 166-177.
De Falla, Paul M. "Lantern in the Western Sky." *Historical Society of Southern California Quarterly*, Vol. 42 (March, June 1960), pp. 57-88, 161-185.
Dorney, P. S. "A Prophecy Partly Verified." *Overland*, new series, Vol. 7 (March 1886), pp. 230-234.
Locklear, William R. "The Celestials and the Angels." *Historical Society of Southern California Quarterly*, Vol. 42 (September 1960), pp. 239-256.
Nadeau, Remi A. *City-Makers*. Garden City, N.Y., Doubleday, 1948. pp. 63-70.
Widney, R. M. "Chinese Riot and Massacre in Los Angeles" and Lichtenberger, H. C., "Faulty Indictment Saves Those Convicted." *Grizzly Bear*, January 1921, pp. 3-4, 22.

Chapter 8—Steel Lockout

Adamic, Louis. *Dynamite*. N.Y., Viking Press, 1931. pp. 101-107.
Dulles, Foster R. *Labor in America*. 2d rev. ed. N.Y., Crowell, 1960. pp. 166-171.

Taft, Philip. *Organized Labor in American History.* N.Y., Harper & Row, 1964. pp. 136-145.
Wolff, Leon. *Lockout.* N.Y., Harper & Row, 1965.
Yellen, Samuel. *American Labor Struggles.* N.Y., Harcourt, Brace, 1936. pp. 72-100.

Chapter 9—Pullman Strike

Adamic, Louis. *Dynamite.* N.Y., Viking Press, 1931. pp. 115-123.
Dulles, Foster R. *Labor in America.* 2d rev. ed. N.Y., Crowell, 1960. pp. 171-180.
Lindsey, Almont. *The Pullman Strike; The Story of a Unique Experiment and of a Great Labor Upheaval.* Chicago, University of Chicago Press, 1942. Paperback, Phoenix P165.
Rich, Bennett M. *The Presidents and Civil Disorder.* Washington, Brookings Institution, 1941. pp. 87-101.
Taft, Philip. *Organized Labor in American History.* N.Y., Harper & Row, 1964. pp. 146-158.
Warne, Colston E. *The Pullman Boycott of 1894.* N.Y., Heath, 1955.
Yellen, Samuel. *American Labor Struggles.* N.Y., Harcourt, Brace, 1936. pp. 101-135.

Chapter 10—Miners' Riot

Adamic, Louis. *Dynamite.* N.Y., Viking Press, 1931. pp. 124-127.
French, George E. "Coeur d'Alene Riots, 1892." *Overland,* Series 2, Vol. 26 (July 1895), pp. 32-49.
Illustrated History of North Idaho. Western Historical Publishing Co., 1903. "History of Shoshone County," pp. 1001-1014, 1055-1056.
Perlman, Selig, and Taft, Philip. *Labor Movements.* N.Y., Macmillan, 1935. pp. 183-188.
Rich, Bennett M. *The Presidents and Civil Disorder.* Washington, Brookings Institution, 1941. pp. 110-120.
Taft, Philip. *Organized Labor in American History.* N.Y., Harper & Row, 1964. pp. 281-282, 284-285.
Whipple, Leon. *The Story of Civil Liberty in the United States.* N.Y., Vanguard Press, 1927. pp. 238-241.

Chapter 11—Race Riot

Cooper, Lindsay. "The Congressional Investigation of the East St. Louis Riots." *Crisis,* Vol. 15 (January 1918), pp. 116-121.
Du Bois, W. E. B., and Gruening, Martha. "The Massacre of East St. Louis." *Crisis,* Vol. 14 (September 1917), pp. 219-238.

Gompers, Samuel. "East St. Louis Riots—Their Causes." *American Federationist,* Vol. 24 (August 1917), pp. 621-626.
Leonard, O. "East St. Louis Pogrom." *Survey,* Vol. 38 (July 14, 1917), pp. 331-333.
Rudwick, Elliott M. *Race Riot at East St. Louis, July 2, 1917.* Carbondale, Southern Illinois University Press, 1964.

RACE RIOTS

Allport, Gordon W. *The Nature of Prejudice.* Cambridge, Addison-Wesley, 1954. Abr. ed., Anchor paperback A149.
Grimshaw, Allen D. "Lawlessness and Violence in America and Their Special Manifestations in Changing Negro-White Relationships." *Journal of Negro History,* Vol. 44 (January 1959), pp. 52-72.
"Race Riots of the Past: A Worry for the Future." *U.S. News and World Report,* Vol. 55 (July 15, 1963), pp. 54-55.
Rudwick, *op. cit.,* pp. 217-233 compares the patterns in the East St. Louis, Chicago and Detroit riots.

CHICAGO RACE RIOT, 1919

Commission on Race Relations, Chicago. *The Negro in Chicago.* Chicago, University of Chicago Press, 1922.
Hare, Nathan. "The Day the Race War Struck Chicago." *Negro History Bulletin,* Vol. 30 (March 1962), pp. 123-125. A bibliography.
Sandburg, Carl. *The Chicago Race Riot.* Harcourt, Brace & Howe, 1919.

DETROIT RACE RIOT, 1943

Lee, Alfred M., and Humphrey, Norman D. *Race Riot.* N.Y., Dryden Press, 1943.
Shogan, Robert, and Craig, Thomas. *The Detroit Race Riot: A Study in Violence.* Philadelphia, Chilton Press, 1964.

Chapter 12—Police Strike

Bartlett, Randolph. "Anarchy in Boston." *American Mercury,* Vol. 36 (December 1935), pp. 456-464.
"Boston Police and the American Federation of Labor." *American Federationist,* Vol. 27 (February 1920), pp. 134-137.
Fuess, Claude M. *Calvin Coolidge.* Boston, Little, Brown, 1940. pp. 202-233.
Lyons, Richard L. "The Boston Police Strike of 1919." *New England Quarterly,* Vol. 20 (June 1947), pp. 147-168.

Russell, Francis. *The Great Interlude.* N.Y., McGraw-Hill, 1964. pp. 38-54.
White, William Allen. *A Puritan in Babylon.* N.Y., Macmillan, 1938. pp. 150-167.

Chapter 13—The Bonus Army

Brown, Ernest F. "Bonus Army Marches to Defeat." *Current History,* Vol. 36 (September 1932), pp. 684-688.
Forell, John. "The Bonus Crusade." *Virginia Quarterly Review,* Vol. 9 (January 1933), pp. 38-49.
Myers, William S., and Newton, W. H. *The Hoover Administration.* N.Y., Scribner, 1936. pp. 64-69, 119-120, 267-268, 498-501.
Rich, Bennett M. *The Presidents and Civil Disorder.* Washington, Brookings Institution, 1941. pp. 167-175.
Springer, Fleta C. "Glassford and the Siege of Washington." *Harpers,* Vol. 165 (November 1932), pp. 641-655.
Weaver, John V. A. "The Saddest March." *American Heritage,* Vol. 14 (June 1963), pp. 18-23.

Chapter 14—Prison Riot

"Convicts Bully a Sovereign State." *Life,* Vol. 32 (May 5, 1952), pp. 27-33.
Fox, Vernon B. "How I Broke the Michigan Prison Riots." *Colliers,* Vol. 130 (July 12, 1952), pp. 11-13.
Martin, John B. *Break Down the Walls.* N.Y., Ballantine Books, 1954. Paperback, Ballantine F77. pp. 3-106. Both are out of print, but the story is also told in "Riot at Jackson Prison," *Saturday Evening Post,* Vol. 225, issues of June 6, 13, 20, 27, 1953.
"Riot in the Big House." *Time,* Vol. 59 (April 28, 1952), p. 25; "Steak and Ice Cream," *Time,* Vol. 59 (May 5, 1952), p. 27.
Shelly, G., and Mazaroff, D. "City Without Women." *American Mercury,* Vol. 74 (June 1952), pp. 118-125.

THE 1952 PRISON RIOTS

American Prison Association. Committee on Riots. *A Statement Concerning Causes, Preventive Measures and Methods of Controlling Prison Disturbances.* May 1953.
Hollister, H. W. "Why Prisoners Riot." *Atlantic,* Vol. 196 (October 1955), pp. 65-67.
"Prisoners on Strike: The Meaning." *U.S. News and World Report,* Vol. 32 (May 2, 1952), pp. 20-21.
"Why Convicts Riot" (includes chart of 1952 riots). *U.S. News*

and World Report, Vol. 33 (December 19, 1952), pp. 18-21.
Wilson, Donald P., and Barnes, Harry E. "Riot Is an Unnecessary
Evil." *Life,* Vol. 33 (November 24, 1952), pp. 138-140.

Chapter 15—The Negro Civil Rights Movement

The material in magazines is almost endless; in *Readers' Guide to
Periodical Literature,* see the heading "Negroes in the United
States," subheads "Civil Rights" and "Segregation, Resistance to."
Book material is listed in Welsch, Erwin K., *The Negro in the
United States: A Research Guide* (Bloomington, Indiana Univer-
sity Press, 1965); available in both hardcover and paperback edi-
tions. Particularly useful general books are listed below.

Handlin, Oscar. *Fire-Bell in the Night: The Crisis in Civil Rights.*
Boston, Little, Brown, 1964. Beacon Paperback BP 197.
Lewis, Anthony, and the New York Times. *Portrait of a Decade:
The Second American Revolution, 1954-1964.* N.Y., Random
House, 1964.
"The Negro Problem." *Annals of the American Academy of Polit-
ical and Social Science,* no. 357 (January 1965), pp. 1-126.
Entire issue, with articles on many subjects.
"Racial Desegregation and Integration." *Annals of the American
Academy of Political and Social Science,* no. 304 (March
1956), pp. 1-143. Entire issue.
Silberman, Charles E. *Crisis in Black and White.* N.Y., Random
House, 1964. Paperback, Vintage Giant V-279.
Westin, Alan F., ed. *Freedom Now! The Civil Rights Struggle in
America.* N.Y., Basic Books, 1964.
White, Theodore H. *The Making of the President 1964.* N.Y.,
Atheneum, 1965. "Freedom Now—The Negro Revolution,"
pp. 170-199.

NONVIOLENCE

Dr. King's concept of nonviolence is stated in his *Stride Toward
Freedom,* pp. 101-107, 218-222, and *Why We Can't Wait,* pp.
35-40, 63, 79. Cited below.
"Instruments of Freedom," discussion of methods of the civil rights
movement. *Christian Century,* Vol. 82 (October 13, 1965),
pp. 1249-1258.
Oppenheimer, Martin, and Lakey, George. *A Manual for Direct
Action: Strategy and Tactics for Civil Rights and All Other
Nonviolent Protest Movements.* Chicago, Quadrangle Books,
1965. Paperback QP 202.

Schechter, Betty. *The Peaceable Revolution.* Boston, Houghton Mifflin, 1963.

CIVIL DISOBEDIENCE

Dr. King's concept of civil disobedience is stated in his *Why We Can't Wait,* pp. 70-71, 82-88. Cited below.

Lawrence, David. "The Fallacy of Civil Disobedience." *Reader's Digest,* Vol. 87 (October 1965), pp. 111-112.

Whittaker, Charles E. "The Dangers of Mass Disobedience." *Reader's Digest,* Vol. 87 (December 1965), pp. 121-124.

SCHOOL DESEGREGATION

Muse, Benjamin. *Ten Years of Prelude: The Story of Integration Since the Supreme Court's 1954 Decision.* N.Y., Viking Press, 1964.

MONTGOMERY

King, Martin Luther, Jr. *Stride Toward Freedom: The Montgomery Story.* N.Y., Harper, 1958. Paperback, Perennial Library P16PL.

BIRMINGHAM

King, Martin Luther, Jr. *Why We Can't Wait.* N.Y., Harper & Row, 1964. Paperback, Signet (New American Library) P2746. Excerpts in *Life,* Vol. 56, May 15, 1964.

Chapter 16—Riots and Protests, 1964-1965

These violence and protest activities were covered extensively in magazines and newspapers. The material listed below is highly selective.

Moynihan Report: U.S. Department of Labor. Office of Policy Planning and Research. *The Negro Family: The Case for National Action.* March 1965.

Shaffer, Helen B. "Negroes and the Police." *Editorial Research Reports,* 1964, Vol. 1 (September 21, 1964), pp. 681-699.

Shapiro, Fred C., and Sullivan, James W. *Race Riots: New York 1964.* N.Y., Crowell, 1964.

Watts Report: *Violence in the City—An End or a Beginning?;* Report by the Governor's Commission on the Los Angeles Riots. December 2, 1965.

White, Theodore H. *The Making of the President 1964.* N.Y., Atheneum, 1965. "Riot in the Street," pp. 232-254. Abridged in "Why Negroes Riot," *Reader's Digest,* Vol. 87 (November 1965), pp. 67-73.

Index